JOURNEY TO PHOTOGRAPHY

College Admissions & Profiles

Rachel A. Winston, Ph.D.

ISBN 978-1946432704 (hardback); 978-1946432698 (paperback); 978-1946432711 (e-book)

LCCN: 2022906895

Lizard Publishing, 7700 Irvine Center Drive, Suite 800, Irvine, CA 92618 *www.lizard-publishing.com*

Lizard Publishing creates, designs, produces, and distributes books and resources to provide academic, admissions, and career information. Our mental process is fueled by three tenets:

- Ignite the hunger to learn and the passion to make a difference
- Illuminate the expanse of knowledge by sharing cutting edge thinking
- Innovate to create a world that makes the transition from dreams to reality

We work with academic leaders who transform the educational landscape to publish relevant content and advise students of their educational and professional options, with the aim of developing 21st-century learners and leaders. We also work with students to publish their books and present widely diverse ideas to the college/graduate school-bound community. With headquarters in Irvine, California, Lizard Publishing works virtually with authors to edit, publish, and distribute both hard copy and paperback books.

This book was published in the U.S.A. Lizard Publishing is a premium quality provider of educational reference, career guidance, and motivational publications/merchandise for global learners, educators, and stakeholders in education.

Book design by Michelle Tahan *www.michelletahan.com*

Book formatting by Obinna Chinemerem Ozuo

Book website: *www.collegelizard.com*

LIZARD PUBLISHING

This book is dedicated to Zixuan ("Stefy") Lin and Madison May who epitomize dedication, multi-dimensional talent, and professionalism.

ACKNOWLEDGMENTS

There is never enough room to acknowledge every person. Numerous people contributed to my perspective about photography. Students, faculty, counselors, and researchers assisted in enhancing my knowledge base or taught me indelible lessons. Over a lifetime of experiences working with students, I am wiser and more worldly.

I gratefully acknowledge Michelle Tahan, Jasmine Jhunjhnuwala, E. Liz Kim, and Jacqueline Xu, as well as my family, friends, colleagues, and professors. With profound gratitude, I also acknowledge those I have known in the art and photography world.

As a faculty member in the UCLA College Counseling Certificate Program, I met many dedicated counselors who spend their life serving and supporting students. Meaningful contributions to the book have been made indirectly by admissions representatives, college counselors, and faculty members who took a special interest in this book's success.

I would also like to thank the thousands of students I have taught, counseled, or supported in my nearly four decades of service.

Isaac Newton once said, "If I see so far, it is because I stand on the shoulders of giants." A few of those giants whose broad shoulders lifted me higher and helped teach invaluable lessons include Elias Tahan, Kendall May, Emily Liu, David Lucarelli, Randy Campbell, Donny Nabors, Michael Kilcoyne, Jennifer Pease, Denise Berger, Betty Ann Klimkowski, Ray Richardson, Matthew Kasdan, Batzi Heger, Serena Chan, Luci Bruner, Steve & Carol Nosches, Briana Flores, Joey Blanton, Shirley Hull, Jacquelyn Lingelbach, and Lisa Blair.

Finally, there would be no book on photography schools and no career in college admissions counseling without the support of Robert Helmer, whose tireless efforts support me every single day.

> *"If I see so far, it is because I stand on the shoulders of giants."*
> *— Isaac Newton*

ABOUT THE AUTHOR

D r. Rachel A. Winston is a tireless student advocate. She has served the educational community as a university professor, college advisor, statistician, researcher, author, cryptanalyst, motivational speaker, publishing executive, and lifelong student. As one of the leading experts in college counseling and an award-winning faculty member, Dr. Winston has spent her lifetime learning, teaching, mentoring, and coaching students. Her counseling practice centers around college admissions, college essays, portfolios, and intellectual conversations about life and career pursuits.

She started college at thirteen and graduated from college programs in such widely ranging disciplines as chemistry, mathematics, computers, liberal arts, international relations, negotiation, conflict resolution, peacebuilding, business administration, higher education leadership, interpreting, college counseling, and publishing. Throughout her education, she attended and graduated from Harvard, University of Chicago, University of Texas, GWU, UCLA, Syracuse, CSUF, CSUDH, Pepperdine, Claremont Graduate University, and Gallaudet University.

Her position working in Washington, D.C. on Capitol Hill and with the White House in the 1980s took her to approximately a hundred universities training campaign managers at colleges from Colorado to California, thoroughly dotting the western states. Later, she led college tours with students and their families on road trips throughout the United States. She has taught or counseled thousands of students over her career and speaks at conferences and academic programs throughout the world.

As a professor and avid writer for numerous publications, she won the 2012 McFarland Literary Achievement Award, Bletchley Park Cryptanalyst Award, and numerous other awards, including Faculty Member of the Year, Leadership Tomorrow Leader of the Year, and college service and leadership awards. While studying Human Capital at Claremont Graduate University, she was a scholarship recipient at the Drucker School of Management. She was also elected to the statewide Board of Governors for the Faculty Association for California Community Colleges, where she served on their executive committee.

She also served as a faculty member for the UCLA College Counselor Certificate Program, the Director of Mathematics at Brandman University, and Embry Riddle Aeronautical University, Chapman University, Cal State Fullerton, and a handful of California Community Colleges, including Cerro Coso College where she represented the entire faculty as the Academic Senate President and retired in 2016. Over her career, she taught mathematics online, on television, live interactive satellite, telecourses, and in large and small lecture halls.

AUTHOR'S NOTE

You are reading this book because you are considering admission to colleges where you open the doors to the world of photography. Whatever route you took to get to this point, you are in the right place. Right now, you need to gather information to make informed decisions.

While many people offer advice, suggestions differ. Friends will tell you the 'right' way or the way their neighbor was accepted. Graciously accept this anecdotal information, pursuing photography with your heart and mind as you commit to learning more.

Dig deeper to consider both expert and current information from counselors who have worked with hundreds of students. Changes in programs, curricula, requirements, and links happen each year.

Doublecheck each program's specifics yourself. Each school's profile information is current as of April 2022. However, since researching this book, changes may have taken place. There are other college guidebooks written by talented and experienced counselors, though none like this book on photography. Nevertheless, I admire and cheer on their efforts.

> *"We are what we think. All that we are arises with our thoughts. With our thoughts, we make the world."*
> *Buddha*

This book, providing lists of colleges, admissions information, and profiles, is different in that it also offers unique tidbits. I hope you find the information valuable. Your job is to begin early by assembling lists of possible schools to consider. Create a road map and set yourself on a clear path.

If you see an error in this book or even a suggestion for a future edition, please write to Dr. Rachel A. Winston at collegeguide@yahoo.com. We will fix the entry with the next printed version. All of that said, this book was written with you in mind.

There is a wealth of information on the Internet with free downloads, FAQs, testimonials, and offers to help you with your applications. Some of these advisors are knowledgeable and provide valuable assistance. Unfortunately, students and parents hunt around the web, searching for a tremendous number of hours to seek the information they need. This book aims to resolve this problem with college admissions data and profiles to make your search easier.

For now, though, we will assume you want to attend college to study photography and are exploring this book to find a program that will get you on your way toward your goal. You are undoubtedly a talented candidate who is willing to work very hard. Creative mental exploration is virtually a prerequisite for photography programs.

As you investigate colleges, you might find that some programs are listed in different college departments – communication, art, design, fashion, or photography. Either way, this book will help you reach your goal. Applying to and writing essays for each application will require research to determine which program is right for you and the specific reasons you are a good fit.

While you might believe that photography-focused colleges are relatively similar, each program's nuances make them very different. These small differences may seem confusing. My goal with this book is to demystify the information and process.

CONTENTS

CAPTURING PEOPLE'S IMAGINATION: PRESENTING THE WORLD'S IMAGERY IN PHOTOS AND FILM

"Photography is a way of feeling, of touching, of loving. What you have caught on film is captured forever… It remembers little things, long after you have forgotten everything."

– Aaron Siskind

Magical, captivating, and thought-provoking photography illuminates that which cannot be seen while revealing stories that cannot otherwise be told. In the flicker of a moment, the camera flashes light, and an image is processed. Photography's role in society is immensely important and underappreciated. Photographers capture moments in life that will never happen again, saving them for memories or sharing them with the world. With photography, an instant lasts a lifetime, allowing people to powerfully feel the moment while translating an expression effortlessly into every language.

Photography is both art and science. Presented in various forms for a variety of audiences, photography presents lasting imagery. Light captures a moment electronically or chemically to rest in a place of relative permanence. While most people think about photography taken in and around homes, activities, and events, the practice is widespread. A few diverse fields include forensics, medicine, astrophysics, real estate, advertising, marketing, travel, fashion, sports, journalism, nature, still life, and art.

ORIGINS OF PHOTOGRAPHY

From the early *camera obscura*, translated from Latin as "dark chamber", photography's development has a long history stretching back more than a millennium. In the early 1800s, though, scientific breakthroughs inspired inventors to experiment with transferring light. However, when George Eastman, the founder of Kodak, created flexible film, advances quickly transformed the field. For much of the next century, photographs were taken in black and white. The monochrome origins of black and white photography led to the introduction and mass use of color images, though many photography artisans continue to take black and white shots. Now, with digital photography's use of electronic image sensors, fewer people use chemical processing, though some photographers continue to experiment with this medium.

The pioneers of photography paved the path for today's trailblazers who industriously foster this spirit using new technologies in digital spaces yet to be discovered. George Grant had a 25-year career as the chief photographer for the National Park Service, producing more than 30,000 stunning landscape images in the early 1900s. Similarly, Ansel Adams cast his viewfinder toward the American West, photographing nature using large-format cameras to ensure crisp images. Today's photographers have new vistas in the spaces like virtual reality and the Metaverse where few have ventured.

Within the past two decades, with the advent of camera phones, nearly everyone can take digital pictures. Moreover, image quality continues to improve. Camera equipment has also improved, taking strides into new possibilities both with still photography and rapid sequence capture. As a result, the excitement of photography continues on the cutting edge of full-spectrum photography with new and unknown potential. However, as you master your skills, you are likely to embrace the next-gen technologies of three-dimensional visual imagery that have already begun to emerge.

USING NEW TECHNOLOGIES TO AWE AND INSPIRE

This moment is exciting. New paradigms of photography are awakening as technology expands. Scientific and digital innovations are disrupting every facet of life. Thus, we live in a time when rapid change will require that we think differently. The future of humanity and all other living things depends on those who can think past today, imagine tomorrow, and solve problems along the way. You live at a critical juncture where 5G, 6G, and 7G will mesh with digital currencies and Metaverse spaces. We will barely recognize our current existence by 2050. Much of that transformation will happen as a function of innovators who will invent tomorrow.

Automated drone technologies will allow photographers to view the world in ways never before seen. Virtual and augmented reality will further integrate into society. Today's pioneering engineers use visionary foresight and transformative power to design digital worlds, opening the doors to photographers to experiment with image-capturing sensory devices, possibly where people can one day feel and experience what they see. Thus, the potential to have a multisensory experience may require 'cameras' with new components yet to be invented. With new technologies, photographers could be on the cutting-edge of how society re-imagines sensory experiences.

CAPTURING MEMORIES

Although most photographers work in the areas of portrait, event, or wedding photography, there are numerous possibilities for those in the professional or entrepreneurial realm. While freelance sports, fashion, nature, and journalistic photography have their perks – travel, glamour, meeting interesting people, and working on a team – there is no doubt that self-employed photographers work hard behind the scenes and enjoy freedom, independence, and self-satisfaction.

Photography once dominated how people viewed life since television was not available. Magazines offered an avenue to see the world. *Life* magazine, one of the great pioneers in helping society visualize reality, brought the outside world into every home. From the magazine's inception in 1936 to its last issue in the early 2000s, people understood the happenings around the planet in new ways. Time, Inc. bought *Life* magazine and now provides *Life*'s collection of ten million images free for use online. Those treasured memories add to the new celebrations and experiences you will continue to have as you travel the world and understand life through your viewfinder.

ILLUMINATING AND RESOLVING SOCIETAL PROBLEMS

One flash reveals naked realities, exposing life as it appears. *Time* magazine released a list of one hundred of the most impactful pictures ever taken.[1] Some of these pictures will never be forgotten, including the terror of the Vietnam war, the self-immolation of Buddhist monks, "Tank Man", and "Mushroom Cloud over Nagasaki". These images will live on, forever etched in our memories.

Time editors explained, "The best photography is a form of bearing witness, a way of bringing a single vision to the larger world." The adage "a picture is worth a thousand words" is never truer than in the hundred images *Time* selected.

Early use of that phrase appeared in a 1918 *San Antonio Light*, newspaper advertisement,

One Picture is Worth a Thousand Words
The San Antonio Light's Pictorial Magazine of the War
Exemplifies the truth of the above statement.[2]

While bombs, genocide, torture, poverty, famine, slavery, depression, and disease highlight some of our local and global problems, photography can bring to light numerous other challenges and instantaneously share them with people throughout the world. We cannot be everywhere simultaneously and cannot truly comprehend the lived experiences of humanity through words or a picture, but we can come closer to grasping its impact. A penetrating example are the riveting images of the Donetsk Drama Theatre in Mariupol, Ukraine before and after Russia's bombing.

People clamor to fathom uncertainties that complicate their lives like political strife, new technologies, environmental hazards, food security, and the impacts of inflation. With a tsunami of sociocultural transformation, overwhelming evidence portends dynamic change on the horizon. This one moment is an exciting and possibly harrowing juncture. You can make a difference by recognizing, analyzing, and capturing images of what is happening today. College academic programs offer a myriad of ways to view the challenges and seek new opportunities by designing next-gen possibilities.

---

1   Ben Goldberger. 2016. "Most Influential Photos." *Time*, November 17, 2016. https://time.com/4574500/most-influential-photos/

2   "Pictorial Magazine of the War (advertisement)". *San Antonio Light*. January 10, 1918. p. 6.

A FEW FACTS TO CONSIDER

1. The COVID-19 pandemic impacted people globally with more than six million deaths.
2. Africa's population is expected to double by 2050.
3. Supply chains, transportation mechanisms, and limiting factors of non-renewable resources threaten populations.
4. Oceans are dying due to overfishing, pollution, and climate change.
5. With the melting of the Arctic and Antarctic, many islands and cities are likely to be partially underwater by 2050.
6. According to NOAA, Miami's sea level is 8 inches higher now than in 1950.
7. Global angst, propaganda mechanisms, and philosophical divisions threaten to widen the fissure between people.
8. According to the UN, one in three people globally do not have adequate access to food.
9. World Bank data show that nearly ten percent of the world survives day to day on less than $1.90.
10. Inflation and financial crises increased uncertainty since the end of the pandemic.

While solving problems in the present, we hold images in our memory, allowing us to see what appears in front of us while observing what we intend to act upon and change. As Mahatma Gandhi explained in 1913, that change in the world must start within since we are but a mirror in the world. As we change our nature, the world's attitude also changes in a divine mystery that stems from the source of our happiness. We can change the world, one photograph at a time.

HOPE AND PRAGMATISM

The birth of photography, from the first photograph in 1826 to today, left indelible impressions. Innovations since that time have brought the medium, once cost-prohibitive, to most of the 7.7 billion people on the planet or 5.3 billion cell phone users. With the Internet, it is now possible to visualize events around the world and share them instantaneously. Thus, with trillions of images taken thus far, photography's exponential growth opens the door to the intersection of hope and pragmatism.

By rethinking image capture and the potential to connect to other senses through new media, the possibilities are limitless. As an experimentalist, you will construct the foundation for civilization's future. Begin this journey by stepping into the possibilities of today and the augmented realities of tomorrow.

There are many directions you can take with photography. The combination of complex concepts that blend art and science adds to the challenge and intrigue of the career. Programs the colleges profiled in this book offer varied paths for you to explore. Choose the direction that makes the most sense to you. The information contained within will lead you on your way.

CHAPTER 2

PHOTOGRAPHY FOR FASHION, SPORTS, JOURNALISM, NATURE, TRAVEL, AND ART

"If you are out there shooting, things will happen for you. If you're not out there, you'll only hear about it."

– Jay Maisel

For the intrepid photographer, the night sky, away from the urban glare, can capture the majesty of a full moon, the dazzling radiance of the Milky Way, or the surreal color combinations of the aurora borealis. On a clear, dark night, the galaxy's celestial bodies glow, luring the beholder with their beckoning magnetic pull. Onlookers do not need to be astronomers to be in awe of the bodies of mass millions of light-years away. Yet, away from the light pollution of the cities is a photographer's paradise.

Meanwhile, a city's twinkling lights, dimmed after a long bustling day of work, retain their magic in a process that takes place around the dials of a timepiece like clockwork. Urban centers electrify. The energy of people rushing to and fro may be hushed for now but will awaken soon enough. This process begins and ends in our living spaces where we, too, dim the lights in the evening and wipe our eyes in the morning, refreshed from our necessary night's rest.

In studio spaces, creativity is unleashed. Photographers, inspired to invent the future, blend vision and wonder with the nuts and bolts of the tools of their trade. Students studying photography are invited to set free the barriers of their minds-eye and visualize what has yet to be considered. Space and time, inhibiting to some, are merely a given entity in which to create. The possible career pursuits with your degree in photography are only limited by your imagination.

On the fashion photography front, Baron Adolph de Meyer, the first portrait Imagineer for *Vogue* magazine seized his audience's attention. With his dreamily flattering images, he broke ground in a field that now attracts numerous people to help capture inner and outer beauty through a lens. Meanwhile, Edward Steichen, whose pictures appeared in *Vogue* and *Vanity Fair*, pioneered a new movement in artistic fashion photography. Afred Stieglitz called him, "the greatest photographer that ever lived." Today, Steichen's legacy lives on as new fashion photographers take the stage with creative and enduring images.

As one of the most sought-after disciplines in photography, translating the vision of fashion designers into print and digital forms, fashion photographers often go back and forth from creating output envisioned by a paying client to creating their own artistic works. One of my friends, who is well known in the Los Angeles fashion photography community, may not make a huge income, but he has tons of fun meeting new people and making famous stars radiate with a unique and resplendent look.

Sports photography is another high-demand field. Capturing the moment of a fantastic catch, an amazing vertical jump, the vision of a runner's split-second photo-finish, or a surprising soccer kick is priceless since it is not likely to ever happen again. However, there is more to sports photography. For example, camera techniques can visually show a runner's speed, the wind propelling a ball, or the sheer exhaustion on an athlete's face. Sports photographers are often freelancers who chase the buzz to an arena for an important game. Other times, they work for wire services, newspapers, or magazines. This position might be combined with desk journalism, so developing your writing skills is invaluable.

Photojournalism is a specialized field. This book profiles some schools that focus solely on the combination of journalism and photography as an artform. Alternatively, you could dual major in journalism and photography, co-mingling the knowledge you gain from each program during your time in college. Most colleges offering photojournalism have the latest and greatest equipment, essential to shoot high-speed, long-range action shots, which, for example, might not fare well in extreme weather. Freelance photojournalists sell imagery for feature articles, world affairs, personality profiles, and lifestyles. Thus, photojournalists present people, places, and events for the consumption of the broader society.

Marketing images attract people to products and brands. With ingenuity, those who pursue marketing photography generally work on a team to conceptualize products and the brand's value, meaning, and messaging. Since customers will view a picture before reading words, the image portrayed is often essential to the purchase. Furthermore, decision-making often happens in a split second. *SocialMediaToday* explains that people engage through visual storytelling, and those websites and articles with pictures receive 94% more views.[1] How companies present their visuals is often the determining factor in their sales. Unsurprisingly, this book is filled with colorful photographs.

Nature and travel photography offer a more exotic view of the world that few will ever see. Most non-African or non-Asian people in the United States will never travel to Africa or Asia. Their only images of these locations will be through alluring photographs or dramatic film. Yet, dreamers remain curious. Invite people to come with you to these often-remote locations through the Internet. Macro landscapes of the sun dancing on the horizon as animals gleefully frolic or micro-images of a rare bird poised on a uniquely colored branch can elicit warm reflections or empowering feelings.

SELLING YOUR PHOTOGRAPHS

A range of possibilities exists for photographers to sell their work. Those passionate about travel, sports, fashion, or marketing, can freelance for magazines or sell photos on third-party websites like Shutterstock, Adobe Stock, Getty Images, iStock, DepositPhotos, TourPhotos, PhotoShelter, Snapped4u, 500px, Crestock, Etsy, Alamy, Foap, and Fotomoto. While I do not recommend any specific site over another, this is a good place to start looking to sell your art. Of course, you have greater control selling your work on your own website, but you need a fanbase first that you can build through friend groups, teaching, lectures, or social media.

Unsurprisingly, more people are purchasing art online than in any other location. The pandemic closed many galleries. Some moved their artwork online and are seeing more sales via the Internet than in their showroom. However, there are also a wide array of online stores offering avenues to sell your art. Additionally, you can also make art to order on Fiverr. This moment is exciting since there is a range of possibilities for your work to be shown and for you to be paid for your creative genius. Art of all kinds can be sold in these virtual shops from drawings, paintings, photography, and illustrations to ceramics, sculptures, and crafts.

With fewer middlemen taking a cut, an artist can go directly from canvas to screen to customer fluidly. For example, FineArtAmerica offers independent artists

a venue to sell their wall art as framed or canvas prints, posters or art prints, or in collections of apparel, tapestries, or tech-centered. They boast of selling more than five million museum-quality products to buyers worldwide. It's fun just flipping through the screens of paintings, photographs, digital art, illustrations, mixed media, and originals. There is even a "Meet the Artist" center where you can post your story and your art.

ArtPal also represents more than two hundred thousand artists. Since ArtPal is a free gallery with no membership fees, buyers can browse and shop without the hassle of some of the other sites. Artists can sell their items or set the site for print on demand. Custom framing is another feature buyers appreciate. ArtPal sells art in the following categories - paintings & prints, photography, drawings & illustrations, digital art, sculptures & carvings, ceramics & pottery, glass, jewelry, textile & apparel, crafts, and other art. Merely reading some of the bios could be inspirational. A few are in multiple languages.

Amazon also sells art. Well, Amazon sells pretty much everything, but Amazon Art is a viable venue for 2D art. Unfortunately, 3D art is not included, but there is a location to sell crafts at Amazon Handmade. In the Amazon Art area, you can click on acrylic, oil, archival digital, watercolor, lithographs, landscape, floral, animals, architecture, nautical, and maps. You can also shop by height, width, color, or price. Since there are so many choices, use the search tool on the left side to help you sort through the thousands of offerings. Merely flipping through the digital pages will inspire you to stop what you are doing and get back to creating your art.

Photography brings the world to people, reflecting the world around us. The real world is remarkably fascinating. You just need to choose the doors to enter.

FOR LOVE OR MONEY
PURSUE PHOTOGRAPHY FOR YOUR DESIRE TO CREATE

If you hunger to explore photography as an art form, you are in the right place. Motivational author, Marsha Sinetar, said, "Do what you love, and the money will follow." Thus, if photography is your passion, you will either make your living as a professional photographer, pursue photography as a hobby, or translate the lessons you learn to another career or field of interest. You will learn how to use various cameras, for sure. However, you will also learn digital storytelling, social media marketing, website development, communication, presentation, and research. Each morning you will awaken with a burning desire to create a special image or simply experiment.

Your knowledge might also take you towards a career in education where you can inspire the next generation. Most people in the world have a camera and want to learn how to use its features. Though you might consider teaching in a local school or college, private classes offer another option. No matter what you do with your skills, you will have opportunities to use them for the rest of your life.

MUCH TO LEARN IN COLLEGE

Studying photography in college will not only teach you new techniques, but also allow you to examine and test your ideas, collaborating with those who have similar interests. You will pursue a curriculum of classes in a creative community that will lead you to advance your skills. Professional photographers who work as professors and have impressive credentials will share their wisdom. You will also have the chance to use state-of-the-art equipment that would be cost-prohibitive if you tried to purchase them on your own.

Ultimately, your portfolio will be your calling card, not your classes, professors, or colleges you choose to attend. There is no shortcut to success in this field. Diligence is required as you differentiate yourself as an artist with a distinctive style. The definition of unique is to do something different.

Get out there and meet people, exploring diverse art forms and developing new relationships with people in peripheral fields. Additionally, networking is invaluable, aided by a talent pool of amazing students and professors who have connections. You do not need a college education to be successful, though it can open doors.

Despite the structure of photography science, unbridled creativity is fundamental to the work. You will learn how to manage time and quickly evaluate the status of your projects. You will also gain valuable feedback from your peers. On group projects, collaborating can be challenging and exhilarating at the same time. Each member must listen attentively and conceptualize options while proposing ideas and creating a clear line of communication. By discussing opportunities for improvement, teams can efficiently and effectively cooperate in crafting the best outcome.

The journey you are taking will have its ups and downs, but you will have stories to tell for the rest of your life. Your education may have unpredictable elements, and pitfalls may lay in your path. Since you have endured a pandemic and the repercussions of a war, you are imbued with a few doses of resilience. You will be tested in your photography program as there is much to learn in a short time.

You are embarking on a thrilling, demanding, and disciplined pursuit. You will work with extremely skilled and brilliant students who started creating complex images when they entered elementary school. Some have worked in businesses and have talents that will blow you away. Some classmates will produce professional-quality work. Do not let their abilities bring you down or make you feel as if you are not good enough. On the contrary, you will add your element and learn more during college. Besides, your enthusiasm will show through in your work and effort. Recognizing your potential, commitment, and attitude, people will be awed at your creations as you also step back to appreciate your work.

Enjoy the experience.

CHAPTER 3

ACADEMIC PREPARATION: ART, LIFE, AND SCHOOL FOUNDATIONS FOR FUTURE COURSEWORK

"With confidence, you have won before you have started."

— **Marcus Garvey**

THE FUTURE OF DIGITAL IMAGERY IS DIRECTLY AHEAD

Technology is continually evolving. A transformation is taking place in the digital environment that is likely to change much of what we know and do today. This is all coming within the next decade. Thus, the most important academic skills you need to learn are problem-solving and critical thinking. With Internet speeds up to one hundred times faster in the span of the next ten years, the power and promise of visual imagery will change life as we know it.

Digital optimization within the spaces of 5G, 6G, and 7G will advance photography and storytelling in revolutionary rather than evolutionary ways. Computing power, many times faster than today, will allow for quick permutations of design options, images, and animations never before possible. Artists and other professionals will collaborate on holograms in shared spaces with members who need not be physically present.

Clearly visualized photographic animations using virtual reality will allow customers and patrons to experience what has not yet been created. Augmented reality will add to this experience by providing the viewer a user experience, possibly, one day, in the Metaverse. Stories will be told in new spaces and environments with fully automated computer design and programming tools. Group members will be able to adapt works for publication or showcase imagery in quick iterations, allowing for a near-real representation as each person analyzes the form and function within a digital gallery or pages of a text.

ACADEMIC PREPARATION

You are headed toward the mastery of image-making. To gain admission to your dream college you must be smart and talented. Even if the admission's requirements do not require a portfolio, and many do, to be successful, there are numerous preparatory skills you must develop as if you were presenting your work to a committee. Plan for your future now. Talent is only the beginning.

In high school, or college if you plan to transfer into a program, you must build solid skills inside and/or outside of school. The more exceptional artwork, photography, and video you can present to an admissions committee within their guidelines the better. Some mix of drawing, painting, ceramics, sculpture, 3-D design, digital art, photography, and film are key components of a portfolio, though not all of these skills are necessary. Some applicants have never taken film or editing classes and are not penalized. Nevertheless, foundational skills in your craft and art theory are important.

COMPELLING REASONS TO STUDY PHOTOGRAPHY

1. Freedom of creative expression
2. Mind explosion of ideas and possibilities
3. Desire to tell stories
4. Love for experimentation with colors, forms, styles, shapes, and media
5. Experience when witnessing captivating imagery
6. Emotional feeling that beckons you into art's space
7. The chance to turn your love into a lifetime career

IS ATTENDING COLLEGE FOR PHOTOGRAPHY WORTH IT?

Photography and film have the power to relieve stress and awaken the senses. School is unempowering for those who are disenchanted with memorizing chapters of text, reading endless charters, and solving problems that seem to have no practical use. Learning math, science, and history present a one-size-fits-all model, where everyone marches in line and dutifully follows the requirements. However, there is something useful, presentable, and magical about photography.

In its many forms, art enlivens. If you have practiced art, you may have a favorite medium to express yourself and define your distinct style. However, with a degree concentrated on photography and film, you will learn many additional styles and techniques.

The immersive college experience will expose you to the practices of great artists and alternative methodologies of contemporary idea generators today. You will discover a wide range of options in each photography class and determine the styles and techniques you prefer. Instructors, guest lecturers, and workshop hosts will help you continue to improve your skills while offering you feedback to go to the next level.

CAN ARTISTS MAKE A LIVING?

Since money and time are valuable commodities, the question of worth, value, and future income always crop up in my college counseling sessions. Consider your future wisely before making such a big decision, though I believe that "where there is a will, there is a way." This means, of course, that you must be dedicated to your craft, have a vision for where you are headed, be persistent in taking opportunities to practice, and have the wisdom to make smart choices.

In a world where social media can connect you to customers, you can show your art through many different sites without leaving your studio, which may be your apartment. You may choose to be an intrepid frontrunner by creating a gallery in the Metaverse and selling your artwork using NFTs, bitcoin, or another digital payment system.

Amazing college professors who are successful in their own right will suggest ways to sell your photography and may even link you to their contacts. In the process, you will discover your brand of professionalism along with a calling card of images that allow others to understand what you offer.

"THERE IS NO ROYAL ROAD TO GEOMETRY" - EUCLID

When a student asked Euclid if there was an easier way to learn geometry, he cautioned that discipline and persistence are essential. Hard work is absolutely necessary. Additionally, there is no one way to succeed, just as there is no one way to take a photograph. You may produce images for a company, sell your artwork, teach, or share your wisdom. Either way, art is a versatile skill. Other professional options include arts management, museum studies, television, entertainment, fashion, education, art therapy, and much more.

You could also manage an art store, create an online webstore, critique art, or help others market their art. You might find that critiquing art is of interest or helping other people market their art empowering. Museums have a variety of positions that require the knowledge of trained artists.

Teaching is often considered a fallback. Yet, many are inspired by the innocence and dreams of young artists. Finally, art therapy has excellent potential to make a difference in someone's life. So many people were demoralized by the pandemic and could not find their way forward toward hope and possibility. You could support others to find their peace of mind. My point is that, as you develop your skills, your talent is not wasted, not lost, not valueless. You can be a source of empowerment and strength for others.

ARTS MANAGEMENT

This field has grown in the past decade as more people seek ways to contemplate life through art. The job of an arts manager is to know and understand art while also having a business sense to manage a private or public art institution. Thus, arts managers efficiently run the business and share the creative inspirations of artists, performers, or designers. With skills in planning events, managing talent, envisioning space, communicating messages, and hosting guests, you will serve society in significant ways. For example, suppose you want to inspire both artists and patrons alike, giving artists the freedom to express themselves while offering visitors or purchasers the chance to learn, identify, feel, and imagine. In that case, arts management is an excellent profession, and it can pay well.

ARTS/ENTERTAINMENT AGENT

This profession is perfect for the person who is inspired to help artists find locations to promote, show, and sell their artwork. Many times, artists consume themselves in their art. They immerse themselves in the vision and technical precision of their craft. However, they are not skilled in public relations, advertising, promotion, website development, social media, and the legal aspects of contracts, releases, and intellectual property. Many photographers want to focus on the craft of image-making rather than pounding the pavement to find shows, exhibitions, events, venues, and other opportunities. Here, an agent may be invaluable. An arts/entertainment agent ensures that excellent art of all kinds has a platform to be seen. Imagine for a moment how many thousands of extraordinarily talented artists exist whose work is never seen except possibly among a small enclave of other talented artists or friends. Thus, those who are 'successful' are 'discovered' or promoted. They are not always the best artists. You might find representing talented people uplifting. Otherwise, you might contract with an arts/entertainment agent yourself.

FASHION DESIGN, TEXTILE DESIGN, AND MERCHANDISING

Photographers with an eye for color, style, and design often express this through their own hair, clothing, or accessories. Often, they enjoy pondering other individuals' attires as models of fashion or ways to augment their look. Starting

with envisioning and sketching fabric designs before they are woven, or designing them after the cloth is created, there is an immense amount of artistry involved with clothing creation. Attending fashion shows, buying next season's designs, marketing outfits, and displaying items in stores takes the flair of a creative mind. Individuals with these interests may discover that segments of the fashion industry are immensely appealing.

TEACHING, EDUCATION, AND TRAINING

Kids clamor to create. Their imaginations run wild with ideas. Self-expression and exploration through art offer people young and old the chance to put their ideas onto paper, a computer, or a still/moving medium like photography or film. Some perform in voice, dance, and acting. As a result, there are numerous jobs in private and public education. Schools everywhere hire art teachers. Families hire art coaches. Private studios conduct photography workshops and training. Furthermore, college art professors can make $100,000/year teaching students while continuing to practice their craft.

In the United States, in 2021, there were approximately 130,000 public and private K-12 schools, according to the National Center for Educational Statistics. Furthermore, during the 2019-2020 school year, there were 3,982 degree-granting higher education colleges and universities – 2,679 4-year and 1,303 2-year institutions.[1] In California alone, during the 2020-2021 school year, there were 10,545 K-12 public schools and another 1,296 charter schools.[2] Thus, there are numerous schools in which you may choose to work.

ART THERAPY

Art therapists are clinicians who support people of all ages as mental health practitioners. They provide services and counseling through the active practice of art-making and other creative processes. Art can be a healing power, allowing individuals to improve their physical and mental abilities while reducing both stress and conflict and improving both self-esteem and self-awareness. Using applied psychology, art therapists improve the human experience in a

---

1   NCES, "Digest of Education Statistics," U.S. Department of Education, 2020 Tables and Figures, https://nces.ed.gov/programs/digest/d20/tables/dt20_317.10.asp

2   California Department of Education, "Fingertip Facts on Education in California", 2020-2021, https://www.cde.ca.gov/ds/ad/ceffingertipfacts.asp

psychotherapeutic relationship. Art therapists must be credentialed and certified to practice in hospitals, schools, veteran's clinics, private practice, rehabilitation centers, psychiatric facilities, community clinics, crisis centers, forensic institutions, and senior communities.

To become an art therapist, you must attend graduate school and earn a master's or doctoral degree. However, there are undergraduate programs in art therapy that can get you on your way. A Master of Arts in Art Therapy can also lead to a Master of Arts in Marriage and Family Studies or a Ph.D. in Art Therapy. Most graduate programs prepare graduates to sit for the Art Therapy Registration (ATR), Creative Arts Therapist (LCAT), and Licensed Professional Clinical Counselor (LPCC).

UNDERGRADUATE ART THERAPY PROGRAMS
AMERICAN ART THERAPY ASSOCIATION

Anna Maria College (MA)

Capital University (OH)

Converse College (SC)

Edgewood College (WI)

Long Island University, Post Campus (NY)

Mars Hill University (NC)

Mercyhurst University (PA)

Millikin University (IL)

Mount Mary University (WI)

Notre Dame of Maryland University (MD)

Russell Sage College (NY)

Seton Hill University (PA)

St. Thomas Aquinas College (NY)

Temple University (PA)

University of the Arts (PA)

University of Tampa (FL)

Ursuline College (OH)

CAAHEP ACCREDITED GRADUATE ART THERAPY PROGRAMS[3]

Adler Graduate School (MN)

Albertus Magnus College (CT)

Antioch University Seattle (WA)

Caldwell University (NJ)

Drexel University (PA)

Eastern Virginia Medical School (VA)

Edinboro University (PA)

Emporia State University (KS)

Florida State University (FL)

George Washington University (DC)

Hofstra University (NY)

Indiana Univ.-Purdue Univ.-IUPUI (IN)

Lewis & Clark College (OR)

Long Island University – Post (NY)

Loyola Marymount University (CA)

Maywood University (PA)

---

3   CAAHEP, "Commission on Accreditation" https://www.caahep.org/Students/Find-a-Program.aspx

Naropa University (CO)

Nazareth College (NY)

New York University (NY)

Southern Illinois University (IL)

Southwestern College (NM)

Springfield College (MA)

St. Mary-of-the-Woods College (IN)

University of Louisville (KY)

Ursuline College (OH)

LIMITLESS POSSIBILITIES

The preparation you receive will not restrict you. One of my students went from painting to game design, which required a year of focused digital skills, but he now has an amazing job that he enjoys. Creativity is fundamental to any area of art. Your options will be completely open, providing you with the freedom to choose.

The scope of photography and film is expanding with new frontiers that offer opportunities never before imaginable. For example, new industries and manufacturing facilities need photographers to imagine and invent advertising, graphics, and imagery on websites and soon the Metaverse. This ever-expanding need is why some colleges like Savannah College of Art and Design, Maryland Institute College of Art, and Ringling College of Art and Design have a dozen or more specialized majors in art, giving students the flexibility to adapt their program with new areas of interest.

Studying photography will also keep you creative, allowing you to explore your evolving artistic style. Photography is increasingly recognized as a valuable skill. If you are passionate about this pursuit, one day, your efforts will bear fruit!

CHAPTER 4

ART, DESIGN, EDITING, AND PHOTOGRAPHIC EXPERIENCES: INTERNSHIPS AND PROGRAMS FOR HIGH SCHOOL AND COLLEGE STUDENTS

"Photography is the art of making memories tangible."

– Destin Sparks

S tart early to gain drawing, design, photography, and film experiences. Internships and summer programs are as important in your educational pathway as coursework. The lessons you learn from working collaboratively and collegially with other art and design-focused mentors may be different but equally important. Historian and scholar, W.E.B. DuBois (1868-1963), a founding member of the NAACP and the first Black American to earn a Ph.D. at Harvard said, "Education must not simply teach work - it must teach life." Your college, experiential, and life education go hand-in-hand, driven by purpose and foresight since life truly is a journey, not a destination.

Note: This list is not exhaustive, and it is not an endorsement of any program. Dates, program description, and program length may be changed from year to year.

SUMMER CAMPS & PROGRAMS FOR ART, DESIGN, FILM, PHOTOGRAPHY, AND ARCHITECTURE

Alabama

Auburn University – Architecture Camp – Creative Writing – Industrial Design

One week – Three Session Options – Full Scholarships Available (apply by April 1)

Students produce designs working directly with professors.

Camp counselors support students with 24/7 questions, safety, and supervision.

Tuskegee University Taylor School of Architecture & Construction Science

Virtual Preview of Architecture and Construction at Tuskegee (V-PACT) 3-hour Virtual Program

Preview Architecture & Construction Science 2-Week Program

Arizona

Arcosanti – Re-Imagined Urbanism – 6-week discussion-based classes - AZ

Combining architecture and ecology (arcology), you can learn in the World's First Prototype Arcology.

Core values: (1) Frugality and Resourcefulness, (2) Ecological Accountability, (3) Experiential Learning, and (4) Leaving a Limited Footprint, Arcosanti is juxtaposed to mass consumerism, urban sprawl, unchecked consumption, and social isolation.

Arkansas

University of Arkansas – In Person & Virtual Design Camp – Fayetteville, AK

In-Person Grades 9-12 - design projects, studio groups, tours, & meetings with local designers.

No fee; completely remote; design camp lessons embedded; students are paired with a faculty member in a studio group.

Advanced Design Camp: students entering Grades 11-12, 2 weeks in Fayetteville

California

Academy of Art Institute – San Francisco

4-6 weeks – Advertising, Animation/VFX, Architecture, Fashion, Fine Art, Game Development, Graphic Design

Illustration, Industrial Design, Motion Pictures, Music Production, Photography, Writing for Film, TV, & Digital Media

Laguna College of Art & Design Pre-College Program – Laguna Beach, CA

Animation, Sculpture, Drawing Fundamentals, Figure Drawing, Graphic Design

School of Creative & Performing Arts (SOCAPA) – Occidental College (13-18-year-olds)

2-week, 3-week - learn Filmmaking, Screenwriting, Dance, Music, Photography

SCI-Arc (Southern California Institute of Architecture) Immersive 4-week Summer Program (Design Immersion Days) – Los Angeles

Introduction to the academic and professional world of architecture – Grades 9-12

Stanford University – 8-Week Summer Courses and 3-Week Arts Institute

Architecture, Art, Drawing, Dance, Creative Writing, Music, and Photography

UCLA Summer Jumpstart Summer Art Inst, Digital Media Arts Inst., Digital Filmmaking Inst., Game Lab Inst.

2-week program - Portfolio development– credit available

Drawing, Painting, Photography, Sculpture, Video Art, Animation, and Game Design

USC Summer Film, Writing, and Architecture Programs – Los Angeles

2-4-week program, "Creative Writing Workshop", "Comedy Performance", "Exploration into Architecture"

Connecticut

Summer Studio: Discovering Graphic Design (AIGA) – Bridgeport, CT

Free 4-week hands-on program for Bridgeport rising juniors and seniors

Week 1 – Music Festival Poster, Week 2 – Digital Media Poster

Week 3 – Animating Your Ideas, Week 4 – Portfolio Art for College Applications

District of Columbia

Catholic University School of Architecture and Planning

Summer High School Program - 2-week Residential (Two Session Options)

George Washington University Digital Storytelling Pre-College Program – July

Produce stories with smartphones, learn storyboarding, and broadcast through social media

Craft ideas, capture images, & create compelling content, including character development

Georgetown University – 1-week – Creative Writing – Publishing

Fiction, Short Story, Poetry, and Professional Writing; visit literary hubs

Florida

Florida Atlantic University – Boca Raton, FL and Ft. Lauderdale, FL

School of Architecture – July (Three Session Options)

July 3-week program for rising sophomores, juniors, seniors, and students in their first 2 years of college

Certificate of Completion Awarded – Enrollment on a first-come, first-served basis

Portfolio development, fabrication, architectural education, portfolio display, critique

University of Florida Design Exploration Program (DEP)

3-week Residential Immersion into the architectural studio environment.

Construction of studio design projects, teamwork, seminars, field trips, architectural theory.

University of Miami Summer Scholars, Explorations in Architecture & Design– Coral Gables, FL

3-week Residential program; 6 college credits; Design, Graphics, and Theory.

Architecture, Landscape Architecture, Historic Preservation; Urban Planning.

Studio experience with drawing, model making, drafting, CAD, visual analysis.

Georgia

Emory University – Atlanta, GA – 2-, 4-, 6-Week Writing Programs

Journalism, Dramatic Writing, Media & Politics, Psychology & Fiction

Georgia Institute of Technology Pre-College Design Program – Atlanta, GA

2-week Residential program – College of Design – Grades 11 & 12 (Two Session Options)

Architecture, Building Construction, Industrial Design, and Music Technology

Savannah College of Art & Design – Savannah, GA

2-week College of Design Residential program –– Grades 11 & 12 - Courses include Advertising, Animation, Virtual Reality, Illustration, Storyboarding, Photography, Painting, Fashion, Digital Film, Graphic Design, and Industrial Design

Illinois

Illinois Institute of Technology Summer Introduction to Architecture

2-week Experiment in Architecture for HS students – Comprehensive overview

1-week Exploration in Architecture for middle school students – studio-based, firm visits, field trips, projects.

Northwestern University – National HS Institute

5-week Film & Video, Music, Speech & Debate, Theatre

School of the Art Institute of Chicago – Early College Program for HS Students

1-, 2-, 4-week Residential programs in Painting, Drawing, Animation, Comics/Graphic Novels, and Fashion Design.

Portfolio development programs; earn college credit. Full-tuition scholarships are available.

Southern Illinois University Carbondale – Kid Architecture

1-week Elementary Grades, Middle School & High School Architecture Camp

University of Illinois at Chicago Architecture - HiArch Summer High School Program

1-, 2-week (July) - HS students are introduced to the culture of architecture, design, thinking, and making.

University of Chicago Creative Writing Immersion

"Collegiate Writing: Awakening Into Consciousness" and "Creative Writing: Fiction"

Indiana

University of Notre Dame Summer Scholars Program

2-weeks HS Students – Film, Photography, Performing Arts - studios, seminars, and field trips

Iowa

Iowa State University – College of Design - HS Design Camps

1-week HS Students – Architecture, Studio/Fine Arts, Graphic Design, Interior Design, & Industrial Design

Maryland

Maryland Institute College of Art (MICA) – Baltimore, MD

2-, 3-, 5-week HS Students – Live instruction, studio time, workshops, artist talks, collaboration, feedback, critique, evaluation

Massachusetts

Boston College - Boston, MA – Creative Writing Seminar Program

3-week (July) Residential Program – HS Students – nonfiction, fiction, poetry – hone techniques

Create & edit the class literary journal and present writings at a public reading

Harvard University GSD Design Discovery– Cambridge, MA (Ages 18-mid-career professionals)

3-week Residential Program – Architecture, Landscape, Urban Planning & Design

Physical modeling, fabrication, assembly

Harvard Summer Program for High School Students

2-week non-credit program; 7-week college credit program (live in campus dorms)

Credit classes include: Creating Comics & Graphic Novels; Drawing & the Digital Age; Advertising, Landscape, & Visual Imagery; Creative Writing

Massachusetts College of Art & Design – 4-Week Art Immersion Program

Students take 3 foundation courses; closing exhibition

Massachusetts Institute of Technology – Urbaneframe – Cambridge, MA

HS Students - Summer Design-Build Project

CAD, drafting, sketching, mapping and context study, historical research, carpentry & construction

Tufts University – 6-Week Writing Intensive

Writing exercises, evaluation from professors, revise, develop papers that build on a theme

University of Massachusetts Amherst Pre-College – Amherst, MA

1-, 2-, 3-week Residential Intensives Grades 10-12

3-D Design, 3-D Animation, Building & Construction Technology; Combatting the Climate Crisis

Summer Engineering Institute, Summer Design Academy, Programming for Aspiring Scientists

Wellesley College – Wellesley, MA

2-week Residential Program - EXPLO Pre-College + Career for Grades 10-12

Three session options; Topics include – AI, Entrepreneurship, Engineering, Medicine, Law, CSI

Youth Design Boston (AIGA) – Boston, MA

Summer Graphic Design Internship & Mentoring Program

Michigan

Andrews University School of Architecture & Interior Design - Renaissance Kids – Berrien Springs, MI

Virtual Studio Projects; lecture; community build projects

Interlochen Center for the Arts – Summer Arts Camp – 1-6 Weeks

Creative Writing, Dance, Art, Motion Picture, Music, Theatre, Visual Arts

University of Michigan – Stamps School of Art & Design – BFA Preview

3-week (June/July)– HS Students – Creative retreat with state-of-the-art facilities & museum excursions

Missouri

Washington University in St. Louis – Creative Writing Institute and HS Summer Scholars Program

2-week program – fiction, nonfiction, and poetry; morning writer's workshops – editing and sharing work

5-8 week – Dance, Journalism, Photography, Music, Drama, Photojournalism

University of Missouri Kansas City – Department of Architecture, Urban Planning & Design MA

Design Discovery Program – Architecture, Interior Design, Landscape Architecture

3-day (July) Non-Residential Program – HS Students/Current College Students

Nebraska

University of Nebraska College of Architecture – Lincoln, NE

6-day (June) Residential Program – Grades 11 & 12 – Studio training; architectural design; scholarships

New Jersey

New Jersey Institute of Technology – Hillier College of Architecture & Design

1-week (July) Residential Program – HS Students – Architecture, Interior Design, Industrial Design, Digital Design

Summer Architecture + Design Programs (2 Start Dates)

New York

AIA New York – Center for Architecture

1-week (July) Residential Program – HS Students – Architecture

Programs for Grades 3-12 include Architectural Design Studio, Drawing Architecture, Rooftop Dwelling, Dream House, Treehouses, Skyscrapers, Green Island Home, Subway Architecture, Waterfront City, Parks & Playground Design, and Neighborhood Design

Columbia University - New York, NY – Summer Immersion

3-week July-August Residential Program – Architecture, Creative Writing, Drawing, Filmmaking, Photography, Theater, or Visual Arts

Cooper Union - New York, NY – Summer Art Intensive

4-week July-August Residential Programs – Portfolio Development, Exhibition, Anthology Publication

Animation, Creative Writing, Photography, Drawing, Graphic Design, & Stop Animation

Cornell University – Ithaca, NY – Precollege Studies and 3-Week Transmedia: Image, Sound, Motion Program

3-, 6-, 9-week June-August Residential Program; Drawing and New Media (collage, drawing, digital photography, screen printing, & video)

Architecture: Design Studio, Culture, and Society, Architectural Science & Technology

New York University Summer Art Intensive

4-week Immersive program in Digital & Video, Sculpture, or Visual Arts

Parsons School of Design – New York and Paris

4-week - Online and on-campus summer programs for students from 3rd grade to 12th

NYC - Portfolio building in 3-credit immersive Design, Studio Art, Photography, Illustration, Game Design

Paris Program – Design & Mgmt, Explorations in Drawing & Painting, Fashion Design

Rensselaer Polytechnic University – Troy, NY

Architecture Career Discovery Program

School of Creative & Performing Arts (SOCAPA) – New York (13-18-year-olds)

2-, 3-week - Learn Filmmaking, Screenwriting, Dance, Music, Photography

Syracuse University – Syracuse, NY – On-Campus and Online Programs for HS Students

2-, 3-, 6-week programs 3-D Studio Art; Sculpture; Architecture; Design Studies; Writing Immersion

Oklahoma

University of Oklahoma Architecture Summer Academy

1-week (June) Residential Program – HS Students – Architecture, Interior Design, Construction Science

Design in Action: Creativity, Innovation, and Sustainability Shaping the Built Environment

Pennsylvania

Carnegie Mellon University Pre-College Art Program - Pittsburgh, PA

3-, 4-, 6-week (July-August) Residential Program – Intensive Studio Studies

Portfolio development in Drawing, Sculpture, Animation, and Concept Studio Art

Chestnut Hill College Global Solutions Lab

Interactive Global Simulation, Electrifying Africa, & UN Sustainable Development Goals

1-week programs – HS Students – Intensive collaborative team solutions to big problems

Drexel University Westphal College of Media Arts & Design – Discovering Architecture

2-week Residential Program – HS Students – Intensive Studio Architecture Program

Visit prominent architectural, multi-disciplinary design offices; meet architects

Maywood University Pre-College Summer Workshop School of Architecture

2-week (July) Residential Program – HS Students – Design Your Future Architecture Program

Pennsylvania State University Architecture & Landscape Architecture Summer Camp

1-week (July) – HS Students –Architecture, Graphics, Design, and the Built Environment Program

Temple University Tyler School of Art and Architecture Pre-College Architecture Program

Architecture Institute – Philadelphia, PA

2-week (July-August) Residential Program – HS Students – Studio Architecture

Rhode Island

Brown University – 1-4 Weeks – Art Themed Courses

Creative Writing, Music, Studio Art, Art History

Rhode Island School of Design Pre-College School of Design – Providence, RI

6-week (June-July) Residential Program – HS Students – Foundational Art & Design Studies

Figure drawing, projects, trips, exhibitions

Roger Williams University High School Summer Academy in Architecture

4-week (July-August) Residential Program – Grades 11 & 12 – Explore Studio Architecture

Seminars, fieldwork, studio, portfolio development

South Carolina

Clemson University Pre-College School of Architecture Program

1-week (July-August) Residential Program – Grades 7-12

Engineering Design, Mechanical Engineering, Civil Engineering, Intelligent Vehicles, Materials Engineering

Tennessee

The University of Memphis Discovering Architecture + Design

1-day – HS Students – Design programs on architecture, interior design, and the built environment

The University of Tennessee, Knoxville College of Architecture + Design

1-week UT Summer Design Camp (July) Residential – HS Students

Immersive architecture, graphic design, and professional practice program

Vanderbilt Summer Academy – Nashville, TN – 3-Week Program

"Digital Storytelling", "Writing Fantasy Fiction", "Math & Music", "Writing Short Stories"

Texas

Texas Tech Anson L Clark Scholars Program – Research Area: Advertising, Architecture, Art, Dance, or Theatre

7-week – Grades 11 & 12 – Residential Program (must be 17 years old by start date) – no program fee

Intensive research-based program; $500 meal card; $750 tax-free stipend

University of Houston & Wonderworks Pre-College Summer Discovery Program

Hines College of Architecture & Design – Introduction to Architecture

6-week – HS Students – Design programs with hands-on studio, field trips, and portfolio workshop

The University of Texas at Austin Summer Design Camps – 2-D Game Design, 3-D Game Design, 3-D Animation/Motion

School of Design and Creative Technologies

1-week – HS Students – portfolio development and design

Vermont

School of Creative & Performing Arts (SOCAPA) – Burlington, VT (13-18-year-olds)

2-week, 3-week - learn Filmmaking, Screenwriting, Dance, Music, Photography

Virginia

Virginia Tech Inside Architecture + Design

1-week – HS Students – Hands-on design studio architecture program

Washington

DigiPen Academy – K-12 Animation, Film, Music, Game Design Summer Programs – Redmond, WA

1-week and 2-week programs, including Teen Art & Animation; Film Scoring

Music & Sound Design; Video Game Development; Animation Masterclass

Wisconsin

The University of Wisconsin Milwaukee School of Architecture & Urban Planning

1-week – HS Students – Design program on architecture, interior design, and the built environment

During high school and college, you have the opportunity to explore your interests through summer programs, skill-building camps, and internships. Try out different fields you might not have considered before. You never really have the same chance to consider alternatives in quite the same way. Learn something new. There are hundreds of career areas you may never have considered. Have some fun while you are at it!

CHAPTER 5

UNIVERSITY OPTIONS: EXCELLENT COLLEGE PROGRAMS FOR PHOTOGRAPHY

"Photography is the simplest thing in the world, but it is incredibly complicated to make it really work."

— **Martin Parr**

In the United States, approximately sixty colleges offer a 4-year bachelor's degree in photography. Many more schools offer concentrations through art programs. Still others provide immersive photography studies as an extension of their colleges of film and media. Additionally, more than 300 colleges are accredited to offer a degree in art. Altogether, more than two million people have degrees in visual and performing arts, with about half specifically in visual arts. However, only about ten percent make the bulk of their income through art.

U.S. College Students – approximately 19.6 million

14.5 million attending public colleges;

5.14 million attending private colleges

2,679 4-year colleges; 1,303 2-year colleges

Another interesting statistic is that undergraduate enrollment dropped more than 4% from fall 2019 to fall 2020 and another 3.5% from fall 2020 to fall 2021, representing approximately a 1,500,000 loss of students during the pandemic. However, with test-optional admissions opening the door to more students without test scores or who test poorly, more students applied to the top schools.

TOP TWELVE UNDERGRADUATE PHOTOGRAPHY PROGRAMS

1. Rhode Island School of Design
2. Parsons School of Design
3. School of the Art Institute of Chicago
4. Rochester Institute of Technology
5. New York University
6. Syracuse University
7. George Washington University
8. California Institute of the Arts
9. Washington University in St. Louis
10. Columbia College Chicago
11. University of Miami
12. University of Washington, Seattle

TOP TEN FASHION PHOTOGRAPHY COLLEGES

1. Parson's School of Design
2. Rhode Island School of Design
3. Royal College of Art
4. New York University
5. Paris College of Art
6. Accademia Italiana
7. Fashion Institute of Technology
8. California Institute of the Arts
9. School of the Art Inst. of Chicago
10. Columbia College Chicago

TOP TWENTY FASHION PHOTOGRAPHERS

1. Edward Steichen
2. George Hoyningen-Huene
3. Cecil Beaton
4. Clarence Hudson White
5. Tim Walker
6. Steven Klein
7. Steven Meisel
8. Norman Parkinson
9. Horst P. Horst
10. Lee Miller
11. Richard Avedon
12. Guy Bourdin
13. Helmut Newton
14. Irvine Penn
15. David Bailey
16. Patrick Demarchelier
17. Annie Leibovitz
18. Mario Testino
19. Lara Jade
20. Peter Lindbergh

TOP TEN PHOTOJOURNALISM COLLEGES

1. George Washington University
2. Syracuse University
3. University of the Arts London
4. Rochester Inst. of Tech.
5. Boston University
6. Central Michigan University
7. Ohio University
8. Western Kentucky University
9. Kent State University
10. University of Central Oklahoma

RECENT PULITZER PRIZE PHOTOJOURNALISTS (WINNERS AND FINALISTS)

2021

Emilio Morenatti (winner)

Staff of Getty Images

Tyler Hicks (Boston University)

2020

Channi Anand, Mukhtar Khan, and Dar Yasin (winners)

Erin Clark (Ohio University)

Mary F. Calvert (San Francisco State)

2019

Lorenzo Tugnoli

Craig F. Walker (Rhode Island School of Design)

Maggie Steber (University of Texas) & Lynn Johnson (Rochester Institute of Technology)

TOP TEN GRADUATE SCHOOL PHOTOGRAPHY PROGRAMS

1. Yale University
2. University of California, Los Angeles
3. Rhode Island School of Design
4. School of the Art Institute of Chicago
5. University of Arizona
6. Arizona State University
7. Rochester Inst. of Tech.
8. University of New Mexico
9. Bard College
10. California Institute of the Arts

U.S. – ACCREDITED COLLEGES FOCUSED ON ART

United States

Art Academy of Cincinnati (OH)

ArtCenter College of Design (CA)

Art Institute of Boston (MA)

Art Institute of Pittsburgh (PA)

California College of the Arts (CA)

California Institute of the Arts (CA)

Cleveland Institute of Art (OH)

College for Creative Studies (MI)

Columbia College Chicago (IL)

Cooper Union (NY)

Corcoran Col. of Art & Design - GWU (DC)

Cornish College of the Arts (WA)

Fashion Institute of Technology (NY)

Kansas City Art Institute (MO)

Kendall College of Art & Design (MI)

Laguna College of Art & Design (CA)

Lyme Academy College of Fine Arts (CT)

Maine College of Art (ME)

Maryland Institute College of Art (MD)

Mass. College of Art & Design (MA)

Memphis College of Art (TN)

Milwaukee Institute of Art & Design (WI)

Minneapolis College of Art & Design (MN)

Montserrat College of Art (MA)

Moore College of Art & Design (PA)

New Hampshire Institute of Art (NH)

N. Michigan Univ. School of Art & Design (MI)

Oregon College of Art & Craft (OR)

Otis College of Art & Design (CA)

Pacific Northwest College of Art (OR)

Parsons School of Design (NY)

Pratt Institute (NY)

Rhode Island School of Design (RI)

Ringling College of Art & Design (FL)

San Francisco Art Institute (CA)

Savannah College of Art & Design (GA)

School of the Art Institute of Chicago (IL)

School of the Museum of Fine Arts (MA)

Vermont College of Fine Arts (VT)

Watkins College of Art, Design, & Film (TN)

You might even want to study photography abroad. Though international programs are not profiled in this book, some of the best are included in the following lists.

U.S. – ACCREDITED COLLEGES FOCUSED ON ART

International

Adelaide Central School of Art (Australia)

Alberta University of the Arts (Canada)

Bauhaus University Weimar (Germany)

Camberwell College of Arts (England)

Emily Carr Univ. of Art & Design (Canada)

Government College of Art & Craft (India)

Grekov Odessa Art School (Ukraine)

National Art School (Australia)

Nova Scotia College of Art & Design Univ. (Canada)

Ontario College of Art & Design Univ. (Canada)

Paris College of Art (France)

2021 QS RANKED TOP UNIVERSITIES FOR PHOTOGRAPHY WORLDWIDE

1. Royal College of Art (U.K.)
2. University of the Arts London (U.K.)
3. Parsons School of Design (NY-USA)
4. Rhode Island School of Design (RI-USA)
5. Massachusetts Institute of Technology (MA-USA)
6. Politecnico de Milano (Italy)
7. Aalto University (Finland)
8. School of the Art Institute of Chicago (IL-USA)
9. Glasgow School of Art (U.K.)
10. Pratt Institute (NY-USA)
11. ArtCenter College of Design (CA-USA)
12. Delft University of Technology (Netherlands)
13. Design Academy Eindhoven (Netherlands)
14. Tongji University (China)
15. Goldsmiths, University of London (U.K.)
16. Royal Melbourne Institute of Technology (Australia)
17. California Institute of the Arts (CA-USA)
18. Carnegie Mellon University (PA-USA)
19. Stanford University (CA-USA)
20. Hong Kong Polytechnic University (H.K. SAR)

Although this book only profiles a fraction of these schools and only those U.S. colleges with bachelor's degree programs in photography, there are undoubtedly many with excellent faculty and facilities, some even in your local area. In my one caveat, I included Yale which does not have a specific BA or BFA in photography. However, Yale has an extraordinary BA in Art and the number one MFA program in photography. Additionally, there are numerous undergraduate options.

SPOTLIGHT ON 5 NON-NEW YORK CITY PROGRAMS

Bard College (private, Annandale-on-Hudson, NY)

BA Photography

Bard College is a small liberal arts school between New York City and Albany. Its mission is to serve the community while supporting free speech, scholarship, and rigorous inquiry. With a campus that overlooks the Hudson River and the Catskill Mountains, the college has an enrollment of approximately 1,800 undergraduates, 600 graduate students, 1,200 in early college programs, and 2,500 in Bard's global affiliates.

Bard's Division of the Arts includes a photography program, developing visual language, technique, and self-introspection. Students consider space and time while developing photography's vocabulary, grammar, and means of expression. Students overcome visual and psychological preconceptions while clarifying perceptions and opening themselves up to emotion. Bard's facilities include the Woods Studio Building, darkrooms, digital imaging labs, 5,000 sq. ft. exhibition space, drum scanning services, equipment loans, and over 5,000 books on photography. Students take one photography studio course each semester and produce a senior project.

Bard's specialized International BA program (IBA) is unique in that it goes beyond study abroad to allow students to immerse themselves in multiple cultures with students around the globe. Students participate in three semesters away from the campus on intensive language trips, short-term study away programs, or international exchanges. Bard also has a focused Bard Globalization and International Affairs program in New York City.

GEORGE WASHINGTON UNIVERSITY (PRIVATE, WASHINGTON, D.C.)

BFA Photojournalism

Students at GW can earn a BFA in Photojournalism, one of the few in the country, or minor in photography. With studios across the street from the White House, there is no better access to opportunities in journalism. Furthermore, the subway line station is near the center of the GW campus so getting anywhere in the

D.C. metropolitan area is fast. Visual reporters and documentarians are created in GW's BFA program.

When GW acquired the Corcoran School of the Arts & Design, multidisciplinary opportunities grew within Washington, D.C.'s natural training ground. With access to numerous internships, many of them paid, students cultivate their careers while pushing the bounds of photography and media. Faculty are some of the most outstanding in the field, including photographers and editors from the Washington Post, White House, and Associated Press. Students learn to be storytellers while also delving into ethical, legal, and economic challenges.

GW offers the Corcoran Scholars Program, which provides funding for top students who are continuously enrolled based on academics and the submission of a portfolio. The award is renewable for up to 10 consecutive semesters.

NORTHERN ARIZONA UNIVERSITY (PUBLIC, FLAGSTAFF, AZ)

BS Photography; minor Photojournalism

NAU's photography major in the School of Communication offers hands-on experience nestled in a fascinating landscape of mountains and Native American tribes. The location is nearby seven major national parks with numerous cultural influences. NAU educates future image-makers in classes surrounding light manipulation, composition, multimedia, printing, photo editing, experimental digital, and film processes. With up-to-date technology, the photography program is flexible and versatile to adapt to the world of new media and visual communication.

Students learn commercial photography skills while developing profitable business and marketing strategies. Students learn the business side of competitive pricing, fee negotiation, image rights, model releases, client expectations, and selecting the best technology for each project.

SEATTLE UNIVERSITY (PRIVATE, SEATTLE, WA)

BFA Photography

Seattle U's BFA in photography allows students to explore various modes of still and moving imagery. While embedded in a liberal arts school, the BFA is a degree focused on camera work. The classes are small and incoming students form a cohort with mentors and a supportive learning environment. Seattle University collaborates with the Photographic Center Northwest. The program includes technique, theory, development, exhibition skills, and access to state-of-the-art photography equipment, labs, darkrooms, and studios.

Students do not need to submit a portfolio in the application process. Instead, at the end of a student's sophomore year, they will present their work to the faculty.

SYRACUSE UNIVERSITY (PRIVATE, SYRACUSE, NY)

BS Photography (Illustration Photography or Photojournalism)
BFA Art Photography (School of Visual and Performing Arts)

SU's S.I. Newhouse School of Public Communications offers cutting-edge imaging, video, and sound tools. Students become grounded in hands-on photography skills while also learning ethics, law, and entrepreneurship. Students can take part in and contribute to 18 student-run publications as well as journalism, advertising, and public relations projects. The Newhouse school provides one-on-one assistance in finding a position. Syracuse also offers more than 100 study abroad programs in 60 countries, with short and long-term options. For example, SU's London program features photography courses, while Madrid and Strasbourg offer options in public communications.

Unique courses in Newhouse include Beauty and Diversity in Fashion Media; Communications Law for Television, Radio, and Film, Multimedia Storytelling, Photography for Multimedia, and Type and Image for Photography. Courses in Visual and Performing Arts include Lighting for Photography, Image/Sequence, Photo Book, Photography and Cinema, Studio Concepts, and Interconnected Studios.

THE MANY ROADS TO PHOTOGRAPHY SUCCESS

There are numerous ways you can be successful in photography. The training you get in college can be immensely valuable, particularly while being surrounded by highly skilled practitioners in the art. There is no one road to get to your goal, just as there is not one goal you may want to achieve. Photography offers numerous pathways and byways. Some famous photographers attended smaller programs where they gained a broader or more extensive liberal arts education. Others never went to college at all. Exposure to the many different forms of photographic art with students who have diverse interests cannot be understated. Whichever road you take, enjoy the journey.

CHAPTER 6

WHAT IS THE DIFFERENCE BETWEEN AN AA, AS, BA, BS, BFA, AND MFA?

"In photography, there are no shadows that cannot be illuminated."

– August Sander

UNDERGRADUATE AND GRADUATE DEGREES

AA – Associate of Arts – 2-year degree

AS – Associate of Science – 2-year degree

BA – Bachelor of Arts – 4-year degree

BS – Bachelor of Science – 4-year degree

BFA – Bachelor of Fine Arts – 4-year degree with most classes focused on art

MFA – Master of Fine Arts – 1-2-year degree earned after the BA, BS, or BFA

Basically, BA and BS degrees are degrees that typically offer a liberal arts foundation along with a major or concentration in a specific subject. Meanwhile, a BFA is considered a professional arts-focused degree with fewer courses in English, science, math, social science, and the humanities. Thus, the BFA is a specialist qualification, which you might choose to do in photography. A BA or BS degree in photojournalism, photography, film, or animation is also valuable.

The BA and BS degrees include significantly more liberal arts classes and thus are more general degrees. However, the intention of the BFA degree is for students to pursue an arts-focused curriculum, and thus there are fewer general subject courses.

Finally, while AA or AS degrees can be focused on providing technical or professional skills for photography, an AA or AS is often interchangeable. Similarly, a BA or BS in arts-oriented degrees are often interchangeable. Similarly, a BA or BS in arts-oriented degrees are often interchangeable. However, a BFA may be seen as different since there is typically more coursework focused on your specific pursuit, and thus, you may have more technical experiences and knowledge than someone who has a BA or BS.

AA – ASSOCIATE OF ARTS

The Associate of Arts degree is typically a 2-year general studies degree offered online or in-person by a community college. However, some universities offer AA degrees as well. Often, the Associate of Arts degree focused on the liberal arts has no barrier to entry, meaning that students can enter most AA programs with a high school diploma or the equivalent.

Some students take a longer or shorter time to complete the AA based upon their skills upon entering the program, certainty about the direction they are heading, and the transfer requirements for the program they desire. For example, students majoring in business may have additional business, communication, accounting, and economics requirements and need to create an academic plan early in their program to finish in two years.

AS – ASSOCIATE OF SCIENCE

The Associate of Science degree is very similar to the AA. However, the AS degree frequently emphasizes science and math and often has additional requirements.

BA – BACHELOR OF ARTS

The Bachelor of Arts degree is typically a 4-year degree offered online or in-person by a college or university. However, a few community colleges offer BA degrees as well. Some students complete their BA in fewer years depending upon AP/IB credit, dual enrollment in high school, and summer/intersession classes. College programs have stricter or less stringent requirements depending upon the school. The Bachelor of Arts degree frequently requires students to take lower-division (first and second year) liberal arts courses before taking specialized courses focused around a major or concentration in their third and fourth years.

The time required to earn a BA depends upon each student's skills and advanced placement credit when entering the program. Some students change the direction they are heading and their chosen major which can add more time. According to the National Center for Educational Statistics, college advisors aid students in finishing "on time" though less than half of all students in the United States who start a BA program do not finish their degree in four years.[1]

---

1   IEC NCES, "Digest of Education Statistics, Table 326.10," IES NCES, n.d., https://nces.ed.gov/programs/digest/d20/tables/dt20_326.10.asp?referer=raceindica.asp

BS – BACHELOR OF SCIENCE

The Bachelor of Science degree is very similar to the BA. However, the BS degree frequently emphasizes science and math and often has additional requirements.[2]

BFA – BACHELOR OF FINE ARTS

The Bachelor of Fine Arts is a 4-year college degree focusing on the arts. BFA students are often not required to take as many English, science, math, social science, and humanities courses. However, they must still complete roughly the same number of credits as a person who earns a BA or BS, and the courses are not necessarily easier. BFA students frequently take general art requirements to lay a foundation in drawing, graphic design, and courses in their specialty area during their first two years, along with basic writing and quantitative skill-building.

BFA students are traditionally art-in-practice students who learn the technical craft of their art form while putting in enormous numbers of hours practicing their skill doing assignments and participating in internships and experiential learning. Students who know that they want a future in the arts often find this avenue perfectly tailored for their pursuits. However, students who change their minds and transfer to a university in another degree program may require an additional year to make up for coursework they have not completed.

MFA – MASTER OF FINE ARTS

The Master of Fine Arts is a graduate degree for students who have completed their BA, BS, or BFA. This degree takes one to two years depending upon the program, coursework, and experiential component, which may be a capstone, practicum, internship, or thesis. While there are also MA and MS degrees, many art students who continue to earn their master's degree in the arts chose to focus on their field of interest. The MFA is an intensive immersion into a higher level of skill-building. However, students who graduate with an MFA have a broader range of talents and experiences than those who earn their bachelor's degrees. While admission into these programs is generally selective, with planning, preparation, and a good portfolio, there are options for you to pursue your interests.

---

2 IEC NCES, "Digest of Education Statistics, Table 326.10," IES NCES, n.d., https://nces.ed.gov/programs/digest/d20/tables/dt20_326.10.asp?referer=raceindica.asp

THE SEVEN MAJOR DIFFERENCES BETWEEN THE ASSOCIATE, BACHELORS, AND MASTER'S DEGREES

1. Starting Point
2. Academic Discipline
3. Time to Completion
4. Location of the Education
5. Educational Costs
6. Earning Power
7. Professional Opportunities

STARTING POINT

Most students who begin with an Associate of Arts (AA) or Associate of Science (AS) have no college credits. Starting from scratch with their college education, they accumulate their 60+ units beginning from this community college starting point. While most students earn AA or AS degrees at a community college, some earn this degree at a 4-year college or university.

The AA or AS is either a terminal degree, meaning that the student will not continue on with their bachelor's degree or just a steppingstone to their BA, BS, or BFA. The difference between the associate's and bachelor's degrees is just the starting point.

The starting point for students who pursue a bachelor's degree may be farther along the traditional 4-year pathway. Meanwhile, the starting point for the master's degree (MA, MS, or MFA) begins after obtaining a bachelor's degree.

ACADEMIC DISCIPLINE

Every degree encompasses different requirements. Requirements for the AA differ from an AS. Similarly, the requirements for the BA, BS, and BFA also differ. With two additional years of coursework, the BA, BS, and BFA are more thorough. The MA, MS, and MFA build upon the bachelor's degree and dive even deeper. Photography majors will not take the same classes as those in film, though a few may overlap. Both are essential to the arts. However, these two career areas are distinct. Thus, the course requirements are also unique.

Furthermore, with the myriad of combinations, it is rare that any two undergraduate students have the same exact classes in the same exact order.

Since the requirements for a chemistry degree are not the same as for biology and photography differs from film, the degrees not only include a different number of credits but different types of classes and program specifications.

TIME TO COMPLETION

Associate of Arts (AA) and Associate of Science (AS) degrees typically take two years, while most BA, BS, and BFA degrees are 4-year programs, depending upon full-time or part-time status. Students who transfer in credits or earn credits otherwise can reduce their time to completion.

Some students may choose to extend their education in photography by earning a second bachelor's degree in another field. By cross-training in film or marketing, students open more doors. Additionally, a degree in business on the bachelor's level or Master's in Business Administration (MBA) may lead to alternative leadership positions.

Time in college can be reduced. Some students have taken AP/IB tests from taking higher-level classes while in high school and earned qualifying scores to be granted credits by the college or university ahead of time. Some students have taken AP/IB tests from taking higher-level classes while in high school and earned qualifying scores to be granted credits by the college or university. Other ways students can enter at a different starting point are with credit-by-exam, CLEP tests, experiential credits, and those granted in the military.

Colleges and universities are keenly aware of the challenges students face today with work, illness, and family responsibilities. Thus, many schools of higher education offer flexible enrollment with opportunities for part-time, evening, weekend, and online classes.

LOCATION OF THE EDUCATION

The AA and AS are earned at colleges that grant 2-year degrees. The location may be at a local community college or a university. BA, BS, and BFA programs are offered at a 4-year college or university. However, with online classes, students have the flexibility to take classes from colleges farther away as well. Thus, the location in which a typical student studies is not as set as it once was. Nevertheless, the in-person internships are often situated in corporate hubs and thus require grounding to a specific location.

EDUCATIONAL COSTS

Since the AA or AS requires a shorter amount of time and is typically completed at a lower-cost community college, the cost for an associate's degree is typically less than a bachelor's degree. Master's degree programs cost more per credit but take less time than a bachelor's degree.

On the other hand, many students can obtain financial aid in the form of grants, loans, and both merit and need-based scholarships. This aid can pay for school and reduce debt after college.

EARNING POWER

Students with more education can earn more. According to the 2019 National Center for Educational Statistics (NCES) data for the median person,[3]

Master's Degree or Higher - $70,000

Bachelor's Degree - $55,700

Associate's Degree - $43,300

High School - $35,000

Of course, there is a wide range in annual salaries from those who have consistent work and are paid six-digit or seven-digit salaries to those who work one or two paid shows per year and earn less than $20,000. Thus, the average seems low when the variation is huge.

PROFESSIONAL OPPORTUNITIES

Earning a BA, BS, or BFA opens more doors than an AA or AS. Similarly, an MA, MS, or MFA opens more doors than a BA, BS, or BFA. Baccalaureate and master's degrees require more training. You can obtain this training through workshops or studio classes, but with a scholarship to pay for college, you might find that the training and opportunities are worth your time. Besides, you will gain additional skills that could prove valuable in your future.

---

3   IES NCES, "Annual Earnings by Educational Attainment," IEC NCES, May 2021, https://nces.ed.gov/programs/coe/indicator/cba

CHAPTER 7

COLLEGE ADMISSIONS: APPLICATIONS, ESSAYS, RECOMMENDATIONS, AND FINANCIAL AID

"One advantage of photography is that it's visual and can transcend language."

– **Lisa Kristine**

RISD, SVA, Cal Arts, NYU, and SAIC stand out for photography programs with amazing faculty, excellent facilities, and easy access to internships. While most students consider New York City for the top college art programs and internships, they should not discount other major metropolitan areas like Chicago and Los Angeles as well as cities around the country that are meccas for artists and journalists. However, you cannot go wrong going to RISD for its deep dive into the world of art. These colleges offer a rigorous course of study and socially responsible projects on the cutting edge of art, design, and forward-thinking optimism.

SCHOLARSHIPS

Nearly every university in the United States offers need-based scholarships. You apply for these by submitting the Free Application for Federal Student Aid (FAFSA) found at www.studentaid.gov. Some colleges also require the College Scholarship Service (CSS) Profile which is available on the College Board website at www.collegeboard.org. Additionally, most colleges also offer merit scholarships. Please review these listed in the profile section. Below are a six schools chosen at random to give you a sense of a few options listed in the profile section.

ArtCenter College of Design

ArtCenter offers more than $22 million in scholarships for students with need and talent each year. Amounts vary based on need, talent, available funds, and recommendations from the scholarship committee. ArtCenter offers continuing scholarships for students currently in school.

Columbia College Chicago

Columbia College offers merit and need-based scholarships to more than a hundred freshmen, transfer, and graduate students. Most of the scholarships are renewable each year with given GPA and coursework requirements. Columbia College meets four years of full-need of both domestic and international applicants. For merit scholarships, creative samples must be submitted with the application. Full tuition awards are also available.

Pratt Institute

Pratt offers generous merit-based scholarships. Sixty percent of incoming first-year students are offered merit-based awards for their talent. In addition, Pratt has restricted and endowed scholarships along with its need-based financial aid program. International students are also eligible for merit-based awards. No additional application is required for prospective students; all admitted students are considered automatically.

Rhode Island School of Design

RISD offers scholarships to students who demonstrate academic and talent-based success and financial need. Many students receive $20,000 awards. However, scholarships are need-based, and international students must pay the full tuition.

Savannah College of Art and Design (SCAD)

Some colleges are exceptionally generous with money for a large proportion of students. For example, at SCAD, 80% of new applicants receive merit & need-based scholarships. These opportunities are available for U.S. citizens, permanent residents, and international students.

Syracuse University

Syracuse University students received more than $400 million in financial aid. Syracuse offers internal merit-based scholarships and supports students in finding external funds as well. Merit-based funding is offered to more than 35% of the incoming class. Approximately 80% of SU's incoming students received some type of financial support. Syracuse University offers a financial aid package to incoming students that meet full-need.

COLLEGE ADMISSIONS:

Success in the Face of Uncertainty

There are no guarantees in college admissions. However, planning is essential for success. The most beneficial advice is to pursue your passions with gusto, train to be the best you can be, take advantage of internships and experiences, and meet lots of people along the way.

Remember, "life is a journey, not a destination." Often the journey is more exciting, leading to lessons, friendships, and unforgettable moments. However, the fact is, in the end, if college is your goal, then you need to know a few action items to remember for success.

Should you worry about grades? Of course. You should also take classes that will challenge you. Colleges pick the best candidates from those who apply. Students must be academically prepared, socially conscious, and talented in a few different areas in which they are passionate (design, graphic arts, musical instruments, theatre, debate, public speaking, leadership, athletics, community service, computer coding, robotics, construction, etc.).

The college selection process is not that much different than companies picking employees. While colleges are more or less competitive, companies may have only one job, and a hundred resumes. Discover the unique drive and internal motivations within you that make you the very best you can be. Be exceptional at what you choose to do academically, personally, and professionally.

Most of all, You Do You

TALENT FOCUSED

Not all schools require high grades and test scores. Many are simply interested in selecting students who are the most talented, most driven, and the most willing to be team players on the college campus. Thus, while you should take a solid set of courses and fulfill the standard requirements, only the top schools emphasize completing a challenging curriculum while earning high grades and standardized test scores.

FOR HIGHLY SELECTIVE COLLEGES, TALENT IS JUST THE BEGINNING

A few highly selective colleges seek extraordinary talent over academics, but most zero in on a student's challenging courses and high grades. To gain admission into the most highly selective academic colleges, you must take the most challenging course load you can manage and succeed. Highly selective colleges want disciplined scholars AND remarkably talented students.

Determine what you can handle, knowing that some colleges with extremely competitive admission standards will only take students who have completed more than ten AP, IB, or honors classes over the four years.

Why would these most competitive colleges require these classes? However daunting these classes may seem, remember, the top colleges have lots of applicants, and they need to draw the line somewhere. UCLA had 149,779 applicants for fall 2022; UC Berkeley had 128,192 applicants. The numbers are truly staggering since neither first-year class will not have more than 7,000 students starting in the fall.

College admissions can feel like a rollercoaster of energy and emotion. Creating a portfolio of talent, training, and experience is just the beginning. Meanwhile, some colleges want to see standardized test scores aided by practice. Applications and essays may seem easy at first, but managing the various requirements and deadlines can be difficult. Therefore, this moment is a good time to get a calendar and organize your tasks.

REQUEST INFORMATION

Almost every college has a location, a link, or a contact us page where you can request information from the school. If you are considering a school, request information from them. In this way, they may send you updates, scholarship opportunities, a valuable application fee waiver, special invites, and other information that could be valuable in the process. Of course, you may not need one more e-mail, and you may be receiving e-mails from the school anyway. Still, I recommend that you fill out their form. Then, since you are likely to be inundated with e-mails, make a file folder in your e-mail for all colleges you are considering. Then, when you get an e-mail from one of those schools, file it away.

STANDARDIZED TESTING

A few schools still require standardized testing. Check first. Many colleges are test-optional. This means that you are not required to take the SAT or ACT. However, if you have a good score, it may make all the difference in gaining admission. College admissions offices are studying this topic and considering their future policies. Much of their concern began with test cancelations worldwide due to the pandemic.

Schools did not want to let students into their site to take the test who may be infected, nor were they able to ensure safety. In addition, social distancing requirements limited the number of students who could take a test at any given site. Yet, for decades, college admissions decisions centered around grades and test scores. This change in the landscape of decision-making has rattled admissions departments.

Meanwhile, some colleges proclaim that test-optional truly means that the test is not required. Yet, evidence proves otherwise. Thus, many students are still taking the test and working around the hurdles amid the confusion. Competition continues to drive students to present evidence to show that they are worthy candidates. In the end, colleges need to make a final decision. If one student has a high score, that student may have a higher likelihood of admission depending upon the admissions committee's decision-making process.

Data show that students who submitted scores within the college's range or higher were accepted at a higher rate than those without a score. Some schools are test blind in that they say that they do not consider your scores. A few of these colleges still provide a place to input your scores. Thus, they are not truly blind. Nevertheless, the decision regarding whether you take the test or submit the score is yours. If the school does not require an admissions test, you can choose to take the test and submit it as you like. If your academics are solid and you are willing to prepare for the test, you should take the test.

APPLYING EARLY

Early Action (EA), Restricted Early Action (REA), and Early Decision (ED)

With low acceptance rates, the chance to get more scholarship money, and chaos surrounding the cancellations and changes in AP, IB, SAT, and ACT testing, students clamor to apply early to schools. In addition, applications to the top schools increased during the pandemic, resulting in colleges needing to make difficult admissions decisions in their quest to build a diverse, talented, and engaged class of students. Furthermore, students applying early have access to many more scholarship options. This confluence sent students in droves to apply early. This trend is likely to continue.

In Early Action (EA), Restricted Early Action (REA), and Early Decision (ED), students apply in late summer or early fall to college and generally find out around winter break, though some decisions come out earlier and a few arrive later. This advantage not only gives students a chance for more scholarship money in some cases but the benefit of finding out early reduces the tension of the long waiting period to find out about Regular Decision schools.

Early Action (EA) and Restricted Early Action (REA) are different. In restricted early action, a limitation is placed on either how many or what colleges you can apply to simultaneously. Many REA schools do not allow students to apply to other early action schools, though some will allow students to apply early to public colleges. Check the colleges to be sure. In addition, some schools like Georgetown will allow students to apply EA elsewhere but not apply to a binding Early Decision (ED) program where the student commits to attending if they are accepted. However, most EA schools do not have these restrictions, and some students apply to a handful of EA schools during the admissions process.

Early Decision (ED) is a binding agreement between the student and college with signatures from the student's parents and the high school assuring that the student is committed and will attend. Each of these parties acknowledges and agrees that, if granted admission, they will fulfill their agreement. There are caveats to this, though you should go into the agreement fully committing to your ED school.

There are incentives to applying ED. Frequently, acceptance rates are higher with ED. Also, at some schools, a large percentage of their class is filled with students who profess their unequivocal love for their dream school. Students who know they have a top choice school, have the necessary admissions prerequisites fulfilled, and are committed to accepting the binding agreement to attend, should apply ED.

COMMON APPLICATION, COALITION APPLICATION, OR COLLEGE-SPECIFIC APPLICATION

Every college's process is unique. However, there are a few commonalities. In 2022, approximately 900 colleges used the Common App; about 150 colleges used the Coalition Application. A few used both. The University of California system has its own application as do the California State Universities and the Texas schools.

The Common App and Coalition App may be started early. In your junior year, consider getting a head start on reviewing what is required. The college-specific questions may change each year. However, the basic application is generally the same and can be created ahead of time. At the end of July, make a copy of everything you have completed just in case.

Some schools admit on a rolling basis. 'Rolling' means that periodically, after all of the materials are received, the admissions committee determines who they will accept, and they send the notification right away. Some students are accepted as early as August. The thrill of acceptance cannot be overstated.

ESSAYS

The Common Application and Coalition essays are often posted months ahead of time. Since this main essay is required or recommended for nearly all Common Application and Coalition Application schools, this is an excellent place to start thinking about what you might want to say to colleges.

In addition to the main essay on the Common Application and Coalition Application, about three-fours of the colleges have their own specific questions or essays. In August, most admissions applications are open and ready for you to dive into the college-specific questions, though many of the essay topics are available earlier, and some schools hold out until later for their big essay reveal.

These can be prepared ahead of time too. One popular question is, "What activity is most important to you and why?" Another is "Why did you choose your major?" A third common question is, "Why do you want to attend our school?" Others you should prepare or at least consider the topics of diversity, adversity, and challenges since these topics have become increasingly important in the admissions process. Everyone has a challenge they needed to overcome. What did you learn from that experience?

Complete the application fully. Think carefully about optional sections. Typically, universities offer you the chance to provide the school with just the right cherry on top of the ice cream sundae, allowing you to share something unique about you. If you have absolutely nothing to say, then leave it blank. There is an additional information section on the main Common App, Coalition Application, and University of California application. This location is not a place to write another essay, but you can include information that could not be adequately explained in the rest of the application.

There are also some schools that include scholarship essays within the supplement part of the application. Start early.

LETTERS OF RECOMMENDATION

Most colleges, though not all, request letters of recommendation from a counselor and one or more teachers. For photography programs, the university may want academic and art teachers. Plan for this. Occasionally, there is a section for optional recommendations too. In this location, you might get a recommendation from a summer program leader or someone with whom you did an internship. If you were in a sport, there is a location for a coach on about a quarter of the applications. Finally, if there is a supplemental application, for example, on SlideRoom, these often require separate recommendations reviewed by the photography program.

DECISIONS, DECISIONS: WAITING FOR A RESPONSE

The period between submitting your application and getting your admissions results may not require a tremendous amount of work, but it does require patience and diligence. First, most schools will send you a link to a portal where you will check your results, though the most important reason for checking every couple of weeks is to ensure that the college is not missing something or has not offered you the chance to apply for an extra scholarship.

Check your portal regularly. Otherwise, read the college's correspondence sent through your e-mail. Waiting is difficult. These few months are a tough period because students want to know. However, the college typically lists the date they will send out the results on the portal. Other popular sites post their decision notification dates too. You will find out soon.

CELEBRATING ACCEPTANCES AND DEALING WITH REJECTION

Acceptance is not guaranteed. The probabilities are low at the most highly selective schools. However, you just need to work hard in school to have what it takes and give this commitment to academics all you have. When you find out the results, you will celebrate your acceptances.

Congratulations! The colleges in which you gain admission go on your list of wins. Check your financial aid and scholarship packages too. Money is often an important factor in making your decision. Consider visiting the school. Many students apply to college merely by someone's recommendation, *U.S. News and World Report* ranking, looking at campus photos on Google, or researching profiles posted on a website or in a book.

There is nothing that replaces the actual campus visit. After all, you will be spending a few years there. While you may not be accepted everywhere you apply, you may decide when you visit that the college is high on your list or that you do not want to apply after all. Understandably, the pandemic's uncertainty added more question marks to an already complicated set of admissions processes.

The buzzword for 2020-2030 is resilience. It is never easy to be rejected. However, rejection happens, and you will survive this. Note that many colleges still accept applications in April, May, and June long after most school's applications are closed. Look up those colleges if you did not get accepted or if you want to

see what other schools might be good options for you. In April and May, Google "College Openings Update". You will be surprised to see the colleges that show up on the list that still have open spots.

WAITLISTS: THE ART OF WAITING

Immediately confirm if you are given a waitlist spot and still want to attend. There is often a deadline. You do not want to miss this. If you are no longer interested or have selected another school, go into the portal and turn down the offer. Someone else is bound to be thrilled by your anonymous gift.

Next, if you are still highly interested, find the location on the portal or site designated by the college to update them on what you have done – accomplishments, awards, extra class, honors, art, shows, or films. You only want to add what they have not yet seen, but if you have taken the initiative to do something more than what you originally stated on the application, by all means, tell them.

You could just wait for their decision, but you are better off being proactive and showing that you really want to be at their school. Students do get off the waitlists at most schools. How much do you want to attend? Meanwhile, you will have to deposit somewhere else before the May 1st deadline. Stay hopeful. This next year will be a significant step along your journey. Relax!

CHAPTER 8

SUPPLEMENTAL MATERIALS AND PORTFOLIOS FOR PHOTOGRAPHY PROGRAMS

" If you can't feel what you're looking at, then you're never going to get others to feel anything when they look at your pictures. "

– Don McCullin

At the top art and design schools like Rhode Island School of Design, School of Visual Arts, New York University, CalArts, Parsons School of Design, School of the Art Institute of Chicago, and Washington University in St. Louis, acceptance is very difficult. Furthermore, the BFA degree is completely immersive. Inspired by the environment, you will be surrounded by students who are creative, multitalented, and focused.

Students must be wholly dedicated to art. Thus, admissions officers and art school directors are keenly interested in the applicant's talent and commitment. As a result, a portfolio review is required for the top schools; sometimes, an interview is part of the admissions process as well. Applicants must demonstrate ability and potential.

CHANGES IN THE APPLICANT DEMOGRAPHICS
CHALLENGES ON THE ROAD AHEAD

COVID-19 shook students as well as admissions offices. Many studio-centered programs closed down or went online. International students left for their country of origin and classes at a distance could not provide the needed materials, space, and opportunities. Many quit and did not return.

Furthermore, some art programs completely shut down. Colleges faced a crisis. While some programs reopened after COVID-19 and some students returned, demographic shifts resulted, including gender diversity and ethnic makeup. Additionally, the decreased population of international students shook art programs. Nevertheless, many students still applied.

Other challenges existed as well. COVID-19 changed the makeup of applicants to college. Many students of color chose not to apply. Other data show that while enrollments rebounded, some programs suffered from budget cuts.

NATIONAL PORTFOLIO DAYS

These online and in-person national events are free for students to participate anywhere they are located in the world. In-person events are often held both inside and outside of the United States. Prospective art program applicants have the chance to meet admissions staff and present art pieces. Students must register online. There are filters with the online registration so you can sign up for events that fit your needs: online in-person, undergraduates, transfer, or graduate school.

In-person events can be jam-packed with people, though COVID-19 changed procedures with limited numbers of individuals inside venues. In the past, massive lines where students waited for their turn sometimes resulted in disappointed latecomers. In some locations, now, there is a reservation system. Make sure you read about any required protocols for in-person events.

More than fifty colleges come to many of the in-person events. Typically, you will have 10 to 15 minutes to speak to a representative and show them your work. You should bring a range of pieces. The website recommends bringing 10 – 12 pieces. Even if you only bring five, you are fine. The point is for your work to be reviewed so you can gain valuable feedback and improve.

For the online events, there are live sessions where you wait in a 'waiting room' queue until you can be seen. You can also schedule a meeting, though only on the day of the event. You may register for multiple school reviews. Note that you will not upload your portfolio. Rather, you will meet with your reviewer via Zoom and share your screen.

These events do not guarantee admission, and no admissions decisions are made at these events. In addition, although the colleges may suggest that you apply for their scholarships or you may be considered for their merit awards, you will not be awarded any money at these events.

In most cases, you will still need to present your portfolio online through the school-determined application portal. Even so, these events are excellent in that they allow you to meet people from various colleges and they get a chance to meet you. Furthermore, you get helpful advice and suggestions on how you can improve the pieces you plan to submit.

ART SCHOOL ADMISSIONS

RISD offers its own portfolio days online, where they will review your work and give you a valuable critique. Hint: RISD looks for engaged learners who will connect with the world. They want art that says something meaningful, evokes emotion, and shares a point of view. Being technically strong is essential, but being emotionally strong and inextricably linked to the audience is imperative. Thus, more is not better. Only share your best work.

Portfolios are required at many art colleges. Since students often apply to 10-20 schools, the effort can be daunting. Furthermore, completing applications and creating portfolios take time and money for training, preparation, application fees, and other expenses. For some schools, there are fee waivers.

PORTFOLIO REQUIREMENTS

The first entry point to art programs is investigating colleges. Apply to your dream school, but also select colleges that have programs that fit your criteria – classes, program requirements, geography, studio space, faculty, career prospects, cost, etc. For now, let's look at the portfolio requirements at a few schools. Start by getting a general idea of what each school requires so that you are prepared. More information is provided in the profiles later on in this book.

CALIFORNIA INSTITUTE OF THE ARTS

BFA in Photography & Media

Students must complete the online application, fees, artist statement, two letters of recommendation, and transcripts. In the CalArts portfolio section, include about 20 images of any medium. A variety of types of work is preferred. Sketches or works in progress are acceptable. Do not use a pre-formatted portfolio as images must be individual, not composited, PDFs, or website links. Make sure the image fills the slide. Provide captions, descriptions, and titles in the "edit details" area. Do not include generic work like technical exercises, figure/life drawings, or still life drawings. You will also submit a 30-90 second video introduction.

NEW YORK UNIVERSITY (TISCH)

BFA in Photography & Imaging

Passionate, creative, curious students applying to this NYU Tisch program must have a desire to push personal and social boundaries. Applicants submit the

Common App and a creative portfolio through Sliceroom at tischphoto.sliderroom.com This artistic review requires samples of 15-20 images, a questionnaire, and short essays. Your body of work should be cohesive. At least 10 images must be on a single theme with a title, caption, description, medium, format, etc. Work should not be limited to a single photoshoot. New and interactive media are acceptable as well. In addition, students may submit up to 5 non-photo images of painting, sculpture, collage, drawings, etc., though not to exceed the 20 image limit.

PARSONS SCHOOL OF ART AND DESIGN

BFA Photography; BFA Integrated Design
BFA Communication Design

Parsons requests an uploaded portfolio of eight to twelve images from a student's breadth of media skills, including drawing, painting, sculpture, design, collage, animation, etc. Experimentation, imagination, and self-expression are key. Include documentation and descriptions of your work and process. Parsons also requires a submission called "The Parsons Challenge". Start this part early. Many students put this off, and either do a lackluster job or cannot pull this together before the deadline. The Parsons Challenge is a new visual work inspired by a theme expressed in work within the portfolio. Students submit a required 500-word essay describing the development of the idea. Two additional pieces may be added to document your process. Observational work is not required since technique and vision are emphasized in the review.

RHODE ISLAND SCHOOL OF DESIGN

BFA Photography; BFA Film, Animation, Video

After completing the Common Application, students will submit a SlideRoom supplement. Students present 12-20 of their recent work on the SlideRoom site. RISD requests finished pieces, drawings from direct observation, and no more than three pieces that show research and prep work. RISD's admissions are competitive so you should curate and edit the pieces you choose to submit in your portfolio.

SCHOOL OF THE ART INSTITUTE OF CHICAGO

BFA Photography; BFA Printmedia
BFA Film, Video, New Media, & Animation

Submit the Common Application, noting the merit scholarship deadlines and specific requirements. All programs require a SlideRoom portfolio. Develop the 250-500-word artist's statement describing how and why you created the pieces you submitted and how your experiences contributed to your thinking. Include 10-15 creative works that demonstrate your potential from observational to abstract.

All media are considered, though SAIC suggests submitting those that are bold, inventive, thought-provoking, expressive, and risk-taking. You may concentrate on a single media or any combination of drawings, prints, photographs, paintings, film, video, audio recordings, sculpture, ceramics, fashion designs, graphic design, furniture, objects, architectural designs, websites, video games, sketchbooks, scripts, storyboards, screenplays, and zines.

SCHOOL OF VISUAL ARTS

BFA Photography & Video
BFA Computer Art, Computer Animation, & Visual Effects
BFA Film; BFA Visual & Critical Studies

Apply through the SVA site and submit a portfolio of 10-20 images of your strongest artwork through Slideroom. Include at least five samples of your photography and video. SVA recommends a cohesive theme across a series of images, reflecting conceptual interests and understanding of composition, light, form, and space. The portfolio's focus should be on photography and video.

WASHINGTON UNIVERSITY IN ST. LOUIS

BFA Art
Concentrations in Painting, Photography, Printmaking, Sculpture, Time-Based + Media Art
BA Art; BA Design

After completing the Common Application, College of Art students will submit a SlideRoom supplement. All art applicants are considered for the Conway or Poretz Scholarship in art. Media uploads of 12 – 15 images can include recent work drawings, 2D pieces, 3D models, photography, video, etc.

CHAPTER 9

POST–PANDEMIC EMPLOYMENT OUTLOOK: STATISTICS AND ECONOMIC PROJECTIONS

" When you photograph people in color, you photograph their clothes. But when you photograph people in black and white, you photograph their souls!"

– Ted Grant

P hotographers often enter many different fields from art, fashion, and sports to marketing, journalism, and law. Thus, photographers play essential roles in society. According to the *Occupational Outlook Handbook*, employment opportunities in these fields are slated to grow from 2020 to 2030 at different rates with more than 200,000 new jobs expected. The median annual wage for entry-level positions is given below. The job outlook for photographers is good with a 17% growth rate. Wages are also likely to increase.

According to the 2022 Bureau of Labor Statistics,[1]

OCCUPATION	JOB SUMMARY	ENTRY-LEVEL EDUCATION	MEDIAN PAY
Advertising Sales and Agents	Advertising sales agents sell advertising space to businesses and individuals.	High School Diploma or Equivalent	$54,940
Archivists, Curators, and Museum Workers	Archivists and curators oversee institutions' collections, such as historical items or of artwork. Museum technicians and conservators prepare and restore items in those collections.	Varies	$52,140
Art Directors	Art directors are responsible for the visual style and images in magazines, newspapers, product packaging, and movie and television productions.	Bachelor's Degree	$97,270
Broadcast, Sound, and Video Technicians	Broadcast, sound, and video technicians set up, operate, and maintain the electrical equipment for media programs.	Varies	$50,000
Craft and Fine Artists	Craft and fine artists use a variety of materials and techniques to create art for sale and exhibition.	Varies	$49,120

---

1   Bureau of Labor Statistics, U.S. Department of Labor, *Occupational Outlook Handbook*, Craft and Fine Artists, at https://www.bls.gov/ooh/arts-and-design/craft-and-fine-artists.htm (visited March 21, 2022).

OCCUPATION	JOB SUMMARY	ENTRY-LEVEL EDUCATION	MEDIAN PAY
Dancers and Choreographers	Dancers and choreographers use dance performances to express ideas and stories.	Varies	N/A
Desktop Publishers	Desktop publishers use computer software to design page layouts for items that are printed or published online.	Associate's Degree	$47,560
Editors	Editors plan, review, and revise content for publication.	Bachelor's Degree	$63,400
Fashion Designers	Fashion designers create clothing, accessories, and footwear.	Bachelor's Degree	$75,810
Film and Video Editors & Camera Operators	Film and video editors and camera operators manipulate moving images that entertain or inform an audience.	Bachelor's Degree	$61,900
Graphic Designers	Graphic designers create visual concepts, using computer software or by hand, to communicate ideas that inspire, inform, and captivate consumers.	Bachelor's Degree	$53,380
Industrial Designers	Industrial designers combine art, business, and engineering to develop the concepts for manufactured products.	Bachelor's Degree	$71,640
Jewelers & Precious Stone & Metal Workers	Jewelers and precious stone and metal workers design, construct, adjust, repair, appraise and sell jewelry.	Bachelor's Degree	$41,900
Market Research Analysts	Market research analysts study market conditions to examine potential sales of a product or service.	Bachelor's Degree	$65,810
News Analysts, Reporters, and Journalists	News analysts, reporters, and journalists keep the public updated about current events and noteworthy information.	Bachelor's Degree	$49,300

OCCUPATION	JOB SUMMARY	ENTRY-LEVEL EDUCATION	MEDIAN PAY
Public Relations & Fundraising Managers	Public relations managers direct the creation of materials that will enhance the public image of their employer or client. Fundraising managers coordinate campaigns that bring in donations for their organization.	Bachelor's Degree	$118,430
Public Relations Specialists	Public relations specialists create and maintain a positive public image for the clients they represent.	Bachelor's Degree	$62,810
Sales Managers	Sales managers direct organizations' sales teams.	Bachelor's Degree	$132,290
Photographers	Photographers use their technical expertise, creativity, and composition skills to produce and preserve images.	Bachelor's Degree	$41,280
Special Effects Artists & Animators	Special effects artists and animators create images that appear to move and visual effects for various forms of media and entertainment.	Bachelor's Degree	$77,700
Technical Writers	Technical writers prepare instruction manuals, how-to guides, journal articles, and other supporting documents to communicate complex and technical information more easily.	Bachelor's Degree	$74,650
Woodworkers	Woodworkers manufacture a variety of products, such as cabinets and furniture, using wood, veneers, and laminates.	High School Diploma or Equivalent	$33,750
Writers and Authors	Writers and authors develop written content for various types of media.	Bachelor's Degree	$67,120

We know what we are but know not what we may be.

– William Shakespeare

Photographers work both in the field and in studios where they immortalize images in a job that is a cross between artist, Imagineer, and digital content expert. The median pay for a photographer is $41,280 for those with a bachelor's degree. Those with a master's degree are typically paid higher due to their more specialized, focused knowledge. The employment prospects for photographers are positive with 18,900 new jobs expected in 2022.

Similar jobs are listed in the previous chart. These occupations vary across subjects since some photographers focus in different areas of society. The fluidity and opportunity in photography across travel and nature to marketing and journalism to science and law to sports and fashion run the gamut of options, not to mention film, television, art, and portrait work. Society has a wide and varied use for the skills of a photographer. However, you will need to discover your personal areas of interest.

The skills a photography student learns in school, including art, film, and computer-aided design are valuable and transferrable to other fields as well. According to the Bureau of Labor Statistics, approximately 64% of photographers are self-employed while 18% work in photographic services, 3% in broadcasting, and 1% work in the areas of newspaper, periodical, book, and directory publishers.[2]

IMPACT OF COVID-19

COVID-19 impacted the number of jobs people could get in photography. A significant drop in opportunities led most photographers to the internet to post their images and set up their independent work for freelancing. The dynamic changed as Instagram became inundated with images. One of my friends in the publishing business said that freelancers needed a "megaphone" or "gimmick" to get noticed. He is not a gimmicky kind of guy, so he searches for platforms to broadcast his work. Thus, the impact of COVID-19 cannot be understated. While the field is booming with more entrants presenting what they created, practicing continues to be essential, and technique can always be improved.

---

2   Bureau of Labor Statistics, U.S. Department of Labor, *Occupational Outlook Handbook*, Photographers, at https://www.bls.gov/ooh/media-and-communication/photographers.htm

ROAD TO BECOMING A PHOTOGRAPHER

The road to success in this industry should not be discouraging since a few steps are required along the way. Even so, achieving the goal is rewarding. Encourage those around you. If this is the field you want to pursue, pave the road in front of you and drive. An internship or apprenticeship or two in peripheral areas would not hurt you in your pursuit of gigs and contract work. Although some internships are unpaid, you will find that most applicants will have one or more. Some internships pay fairly well. Even if you will ultimately be a freelancer, you might find parallel bread and butter professions while you fine-tune your craft.

If you are serious, you will make a fantastic career out of your pursuit. Initiative-taking persistence, talent, creativity, and moxie can get you into your desired college program and career. You may have to start at the very bottom of the ladder, but you can climb the rungs methodically one by one.

Companies want to know employees' work ethic, personality, and professionalism. An internship allows you to get to know the corporate climate better and allows others to get to know you better too. Thus, many companies hire the interns they feel are the best fit rather than choosing candidates from the piles of resumes that have been submitted.

Education unlocks doors no matter which direction your career takes you. Whatever direction you pursue, if you lay a foundation, undaunted by the competition, and are unafraid of starting at the bottom, you will do fine. Hard work and creativity go a long way in this industry. Start by getting a solid education.

MANAGEMENT AND EMPLOYEE RETENTION

Skills to Know: Management, Human Resources, Social Consciousness, Ethics

One of the most significant challenges facing employers in the years from 2022 - 2030 will be locating and retaining talent. The pandemic slowed education and learning with online classes, reduced access to faculty/advising, limited access to labs, inability to attend workshops, retail closures, and fewer conferences, meetings, and shows. Health concerns rose to the top of importance as did financial stress, job uncertainty, and social consciousness.

Many students chose to work rather than study and start online stores when they could not access locations for community service or continue with their sport, instrument, or hobbies. With the changes in lifestyle and fears about health, safety, and wellness, many bright and talented students developed a fearless sense of autonomy and independence, while for others, the necessary skills ordinarily developed in school were fraught by limitations.

Finding talent within the changing hiring atmosphere will require new skills to retain staff. Employees are increasingly looking elsewhere for a better opportunity. This development will require managers to earn and harness employee trust and loyalty.

The digital workforce has also placed demands on human resources. While many companies want their employees to work in-person, the convenience of working at home and the drudgery of commuting to work have created an environment where employees seek greater flexibility. Changes are coming. The employee talent challenge is likely to create a more global workforce where companies look for less expensive online talent from a pool of eager workers in other countries.

CHAPTER 10

NEXT STEPS: PREPARATION AND REAL-WORLD SKILLS

"The camera is an excuse to be someplace you otherwise don't belong. It gives me both a point of connection and a point of separation."

– Susan Meiselas

Each photograph is a lasting impression, a moment captured today and viewed tomorrow. As a photographer, you will experience a dynamic, multidimensional world. In some careers, repetitive tasks and uninspiring projects lead employees to loathe their jobs and tick off minutes until their day is done. Yet, your life will undoubtedly be different and ever-changing since the world around you changes moment to moment. Photography is about creating, inventing, and energizing. Over time, whichever area of photography becomes your focus, you will earn your way to a career of endless possibilities.

German fashion designer and photographer Karl Lagerfeld shared, "What I like about photographs is that they capture a moment that's gone forever, impossible to reproduce." Today is a precious moment. As you contemplate college choices and tomorrow's future, you will explore your passion, open doors you never expected, and discover opportunities that will tantalize and challenge you along the way. You will also find ways to serve humanity. As such, you will point and shoot to capture a new, exciting, and eclectic way of life.

Contemplate your work, always critiquing yourself. You will enhance and uplift your world by adding intrigue. Spend time thinking, even though time sometimes seems short. You may feel as if time slips through your fingers like sand in an hourglass. Resist the temptation to post, remembering that imaginative, captivating pictures move people deeply. While you can quickly post your images for the world to see, the truly magical pictures are created when time stands still and you immerse yourself in a creative state.

Bring people into your world so they can see what you see through the lens. You get to tell motivational stories each day which may make all the difference in a person's life. You may capture a leaping basketball star shooting an incredible basket or a bruised child surrounded by his friends on a soccer field. You might catch a swirl of color on a dangling scarf or exquisitely designed boots made from compostable fabric. You might catch the heart-wrenching emotion of a refugee whose family was just murdered or the agony of extreme poverty among the elderly. Societal purpose and technological innovation may change, though vision and service will never go out of style.

Attending a respected school can help you get noticed. Your next steps are aided by connections offered by professors, classmates, and alumni. Networking at events is also an excellent way to discover opportunities. Shows, displays, and contests in school, out of school, in the summer, or through social media can help you get noticed.

Throughout your varied experiences, you will meet other photographers who may recommend you or inform you about open positions or contract opportunities, even some that are not publicly announced. In addition, many schools have a culminating event where you can put your best foot forward and showcase your work. Exposure to industry professionals can open new doors while interacting with people online or in-person will allow you to maintain those connections.

Autonomy and freedom to choose the jobs you take by venturing out on your own may seem alluring, but freelancing may result in uncertainty or even career limitations. As a result, companies often choose seasoned professionals with work experience in other firms. However, there are ways to mitigate against the lean times of solo work. A few options include demonstrating mastery, producing amazing work, resolving client problems, aligning ideologies, and initially charging less. Despite challenges, put yourself out there.

You could wait for the phone to ring to be discovered. However, you should post regularly and be out and about for that to happen. Some individuals pine away, hoping to be selected and deciding which organization would be a perfect fit. Others decide that they only want to work at a specific firm or location. Still others determine that they will work for themselves and be their own boss. Yet, sometimes taking any position at the start is a stepping stone to your dream life, commitment to service, and opportunity to put your unique mark on society.

BOLD NETWORKING

Networking takes social skills and a bit of moxie. From elevator speeches and professional encounters to interviews and masterclasses, your job is to find a way to get your work in front of people and have them see your talent and your potential to contribute. You have something special and fresh ideas. Finally, there is a professional entity that will welcome your style, ingenuity, discipline, and impact.

How can you be recognized? Meet people; hand out your resume; give them your business card; ask for their business card; follow up; ask if you can call or meet them, even when approaching these professionals may seem uncomfortable. Stay in touch with people you meet, even if it is just happenstance or serendipity. Keep a log with each person's phone, e-mail, identifying information, and both date and location where you met. You never know when you will need it.

If you meet people professionally at a masterclass or workshop, even if you do not exchange information, you will recognize them at a later date. They may recognize you in a future event too. Keep training. You should always seek ways to improve, irrespective of your experience. Lifelong learning improves your ability to maintain up-to-date skills and transition to new ventures. The outside world's perspective changes more quickly with social media's instant influences.

Though you should not take workshops just for the sake of meeting people, when you attend, be present in your quest to lead, serve, and envision. If your focus is not on your improvement or development, you may appear insincere in your intentions. However, workshops, conferences, and contests can allow others to see your purpose, vision, and talent.

Big-ticket training does not always mean better trainers or opportunities. Find time to visit museums, survey your surroundings, and notice cultural changes. While gathering new thoughts, remember humility and open-mindedness go a long way. Defer to the wise and listen. There is much you can learn.

STAY IN TOUCH

Do not annoy busy people, but you can keep in touch every couple of months. Communicating more frequently is overwhelming. However, life is long. People who grow with their craft transition fluidly through life's career phases. In photography, contacts are essential in all phases of your career. Also, do not be surprised. Many go-getters seeking to gain a coveted contract do the following:

1. Speak at Chamber of Commerce meetings.
2. Attend photography or creative software trade shows.
3. Gain a following on Instagram and Pinterest.
4. Write a newsletter and publish it on LinkedIn and other sources.
5. Link your work to Facebook, Twitter, and other social media.
6. Enter in design contests.
7. Join professional associations.
8. Attend social gatherings of potential customers.
9. Keep in touch with your professors.
10. Stay involved with your alumni associations.

Friendships matter. Become lifelong colleagues by finding friends who share mutual interests and offer a sounding board or connections to new opportunities. People tend to stay in touch with "important" people. Note to self: Your contemporaries or peers are important people...although possibly not yet. As you form lists of contacts, you are likely to know these people throughout your career.

Be audacious while also being authentic. Networking can sometimes appear fake or forced as if you are going out on a hunt to find people for your own benefit. Worse, the act of networking can appear like stalking for those who incessantly attempt to connect.

The mental image of this type of 'networking' conjures the vision of people congregating at meetings. Friendships and the mutual support of allies can be enormously helpful, though 20,000 or even 200,000 followers on your website do not mean you are popular. However, you can have unexpected meaningful exchanges if you get out, meet people, and live life.

There are times when deeply moving, casual conversations in non-professional settings could also turn into connections. Do not lose touch with people or burn bridges along the way. This industry is not that big, especially whatever subspecialty you choose. You will continually see extraordinary talent. You never know. They may contact you to collaborate one day or meet for coffee at an event.

COLLEGE AND CAREER CENTERS

Although photography programs often have internal connections to help you secure an internship or job, you might also speak to someone at your campus career center. They often have interesting and possibly different prospects you might not get elsewhere. In addition, there may be a specific career liaison for their art programs. Connect with them for help in your search process. Besides, you might want a related job that utilizes your creative, design, problem-solving, and presentation skills.

Companies that attend photography shows often hire graduates whose energy, initiative, and cutting-edge knowledge are invaluable. Camera, filmmaking, and design software companies also appreciate those who can demonstrate their products. Adobe, for example, has more than 24,000 employees worldwide. These jobs may or may not be your dream job now, but you might be surprised where the position may lead you, and sometimes you just need employment to earn money and get yourself on your feet.

Career center coordinators often have excellent ideas of alternative options you may have never considered. Furthermore, they can assist you with creating a professional resume and cover letters for specific industries that are different from the ones you have for photography.

They may also connect you with past graduates in the industry who make excellent connections. Some of them may have been in your program and have been through the ropes, know a few people, and may be able to get you an interview or invite you to an industry event. Any contact may help you get your foot in the door or find a job to make money in the meantime.

LINKEDIN

LinkedIn is especially helpful for career searches. You can find numerous influential contacts on LinkedIn. After interviews or events, connect with each person you met on LinkedIn. Keep a contact list of individuals you get to know in your area of interest. Do not constantly try to connect with people you do not really know. However, if you have made the connection, occasionally keep in touch.

While some LinkedIn message boxes may be full and you may not get a reply, you can try. Some people have tens of thousands of LinkedIn followers. I have about 20,000 'contacts', which does not necessitate that I am important. Remember that a paycheck or lots of friends does not make you more worthy or successful. Worth and value emanate from within your heart. Occasionally, you hit on a lucky break. Though I do not have time to communicate with everyone, I have connected with some of my most inspiring authors, advisors, and intellectual leaders through LinkedIn.

FINALLY

Most people are willing to help you. Five percent will not. Thus, you have a 19 out of 20 chance of interacting with decent people who have the time and will give you advice. Don't lose faith in humanity just because you run into a few people who are too busy to stop for you or are too self-absorbed that they cannot answer your question.

Remember that talent is only the beginning. You need to sell yourself. As you organize your goals and responsibilities, remember to think one step ahead of where you want to be by making a game plan. Since actions speak louder than

words, take action without complaining and spread kindness along the way. Burned bridges are tough to reconstruct.

Honesty and trustworthiness are worth more than any physical object. Earn this by working hard, being efficient, and telling the truth. Acting professionally in your words and deeds is essential. Put away all distractions and focus on your tasks. Texts and social media take a surprising amount of time. Every action you take is a stepping stone to your future. Discipline is achieved by creating a goal and making it happen.

A nice note, card, or gift reminds people you are thinking about them, even when you are incredibly busy. Good friends who have your best interest may know doors that are not yet open for you. Keep in touch with them.

So, go on a walk, meet people, and live fully. Serendipity happens when you live life. However, your education is immensely valuable. Success happens when preparation meets opportunity. Thus, preparation is the best way to generate luck. Finally, even the most disciplined person can be lazy or inefficient. Fight this. Stay active. Make your life happen for you. Here are a few things to remember as you go out to pursue your dreams.

- Work ethic is everything.
- Excellence is expected.
- Learn what you do not know on your own time.
- Come to work prepared.
- Take constructive criticism well.
- Be humble and respectful
- Keep your cool under pressure.
- Avoid being timid.
- Stay on task.
- Come early.
- Stay late.
- Take your work seriously.
- Do more than expected.
- Be thoughtful and courteous.
- Read your e-mail/texts after hours in case something is important.
- Ask questions. No question is too stupid.
- The only stupid question is the one that is never asked.
- Maintain a clean workspace.
- Dress and act professionally.
- Don't gossip or complain.
- Play when you are done.
- Study hard, play hard – in that order.
- Avoid frustrating your phenomenally busy supervisor.
- Be straightforward, and don't beat around the bush.

You've Got This!

4
Regions

51
Programs

COLLEGE PROFILES AND REQUIREMENTS

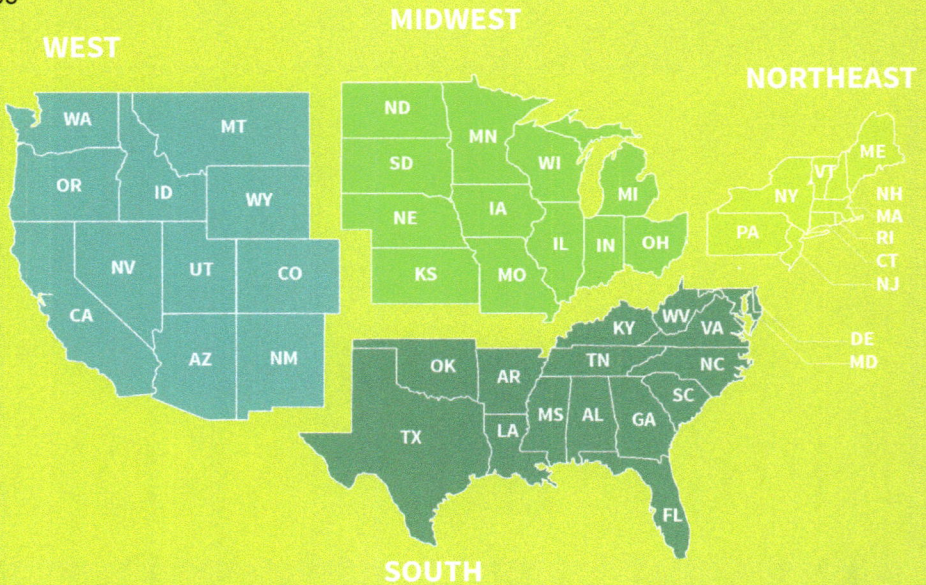

WEST
MIDWEST
NORTHEAST

WA
MT
ND
MN
WI
MI
ME
VT
NY
NH
MA
RI
CT
NJ
OR
ID
WY
SD
IA
PA
NV
UT
CO
NE
IL
IN
OH
CA
MO
KS
AZ
NM
OK
AR
KY
WV
VA
DE
MD
TN
NC
TX
LA
MS
AL
GA
SC
FL

SOUTH

PROGRAMS BY REGION
U.S. CENSUS BUREAU CLASSIFICATIONS

REGION 1 – NORTHEAST

Connecticut, Maine, Massachusetts, New Hampshire, New Jersey, New York, Pennsylvania, Rhode Island, and Vermont

REGION 2 – MIDWEST

Illinois, Indiana, Iowa, Kansas, Michigan, Minnesota, Missouri, Nebraska, North Dakota, Ohio, South Dakota, and Wisconsin

REGION 3 – SOUTH

Alabama, Arkansas, Delaware, District of Columbia, Florida, Georgia, Kentucky, Louisiana, Maryland, Mississippi, North Carolina, Oklahoma, South Carolina, Tennessee, Texas, Virginia, and West Virginia

REGION 4 – WEST

Alaska, Arizona, California, Colorado, Hawaii, Idaho, Montana, Nevada, New Mexico, Oregon, Utah, Washington, and Wyoming

LIST OF PHOTOGRAPHY PROGRAMS

The 51 programs listed in the following pages include profiles of the top undergraduate photography programs as of April 2022 along with additional college photography programs that offer closely related degrees. Although many students interested in photography are often also interested in film production, direction, editing, animation, and screenwriting, those schools are listed in other books.

Photography is not for everyone. Although immensely rewarding, success requires initiative. Some students dual major for greater flexibility. In college, students discover their priorities, commitments, and perseverance. A few choose an alternative path somewhere down the road.

Thus, this book provides you with lists for other areas of art programs so you can explore those options. Keep the book handy. Even after you begin college, you may find that the summer and alternative college programs are helpful.

Creating lists is often tedious and cumbersome. These lists were gathered to help you with this task.

Descriptions of the college programs, tuition, requirements, and deadlines are accurate as of April 2022. However, the requirements may have changed by the time you purchase this book. Nevertheless, this information is a great place to start!

Note: To simplify the text and fit information into the charts and descriptions, abbreviations were used as well as shortened sentences and acronyms.

CHAPTER 11

REGION ONE

NORTHEAST

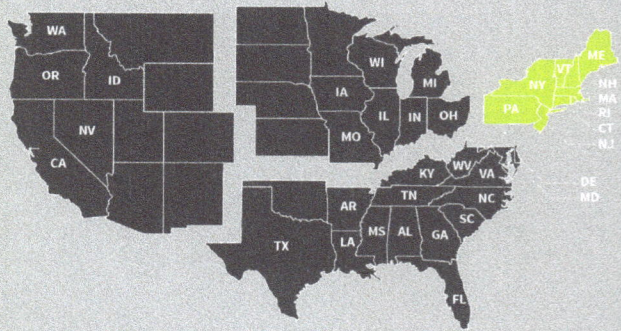

15 Programs | **9** States

1. MA - Massachusetts College of Art & Design
2. NY - Fashion Institute of Technology
3. NY - New York University
4. NY - Parsons School of Design
5. NY - Pratt Institute
6. NY - Rochester Institute of Technology
7. NY - School of Visual Arts
8. NY - St. John's University
9. NY - SUNY Buffalo
10. NY - Syracuse University
11. PA - Drexel University
12. PA - Temple University
13. PA - University of the Arts
14. RI - Providence College
15. RI - Rhode Island School of Design

School	Avg. GPA, SAT Evidence-Based Reading Writing (ERW), SAT Math (M), and ACT Composite (C) Early Decision (ED): Yes/No	Admission Statistics	Program(s)	Portfolio Required (req.)
Massachusetts College of Art & Design 621 Huntington Ave, Boston, MA 02115	GPA: N/A SAT (ERW): N/A SAT (M): N/A ACT (C): N/A *Test-optional ED: No	Admit Rate: 70% Undergrad Enrollment: 1,770 Total Enrollment: 1,894	BFA Photography	Portfolio req.
Fashion Institute of Technology (FIT) 227 West 27th Street, New York City, NY 10001	GPA: N/A SAT (ERW): N/A SAT (M): N/A ACT (C): N/A *FIT is test optional. ED: No	Admit Rate: 59% Undergrad Enrollment: 7,959 Total Enrollment: 8,191	BFA Photography and Related Media	Portfolio req.
New York University (NYU) 27 West 4th Street, New York, NY 10014	GPA: 3.71 SAT (ERW): 670-740 SAT (M): 700-800 ACT (C): 31-34 ED: Yes	Overall College Admit Rate: 21% Undergrad Enrollment: 27,444 Total Enrollment: 52,775	BFA Photography & Imaging	Portfolio req.
Parsons - The New School 66 Fifth Avenue, New York, NY 10011	GPA: N/A SAT (ERW): 580-680 SAT (M): 560-680 ACT (C): 26-30 ED: No	Admit Rate: 69% Undergrad Enrollment: 6,399 Total Enrollment: 9,047	BFA Photography	Portfolio req.

School	Avg. GPA, SAT Evidence-Based Reading Writing (ERW), SAT Math (M), and ACT Composite (C) Early Decision (ED): Yes/No	Admission Statistics	Program(s)	Portfolio Required (req.)
Pratt Institute 200 Willoughby Avenue, Brooklyn, NY 11205	GPA: 3.82 SAT (ERW): 570-660 SAT (M): 550-680 ACT (C): 25-30 ED: No	Admit Rate: 66% Undergrad Enrollment: 3,122 Total Enrollment: 4,353	BFA Photography	Portfolio req.
Rochester Institute of Technology 1 Lomb Memorial Dr, Rochester, NY 14623	GPA: 3.7 SAT (ERW): 600-690 SAT (M): 620-730 ACT (C): 28-33 ED: No	Overall College Admit Rate: 74% Undergrad Enrollment: 13,142 Total Enrollment: 16,158	BFA Photographic and Imaging Arts	Portfolio not req.
School of Visual Arts (SVA) 209 East 23rd Street, New York, NY 10010	GPA: 3.91 SAT (ERW): 545-650 SAT (M): 530-680 ACT (C): 23-27 ED: No	Overall College Admit Rate: 72% Undergrad Enrollment: 3,192 Total Enrollment: 3,692	BFA Photography and Video	Portfolio req.
St. John's University 8000 Utopia Pkwy, Queens, NY 11439	GPA: N/A SAT (ERW): 540-640 SAT (M): 540-660 ACT (C): 23-29 ED: Yes	Overall College Admit Rate: 75% Undergrad Enrollment: 15,693 Total Enrollment: 20,143	BFA Photography	Portfolio req.

NORTHEAST

PHOTOGRAPHY PROGRAMS

School	Avg. GPA, SAT Evidence-Based Reading Writing (ERW), SAT Math (M), and ACT Composite (C) Early Decision (ED): Yes/No	Admission Statistics	Program(s)	Portfolio Required (req.)
SUNY Buffalo 285 Alumni Arena, North Campus, Buffalo, New York 14260	GPA: 3.7 SAT (ERW): 560-640 SAT (M): 580-670 ACT (C): 23-29 ED: No	Overall College Admit Rate: 37% Undergrad Enrollment: 22,306 Total Enrollment: 32,347	BFA Fine Arts, Concentration: Photography	Portfolio not req.
Syracuse University 401 University Place, Syracuse, NY 13244-2130	GPA: 3.67 SAT (ERW): N/A SAT (M): N/A ACT (C): N/A ED: Yes	Overall College Admit Rate: 69% Undergrad Enrollment: 14,479 Total Enrollment: 21,322	BA Photography BFA Art Photography	Portfolio req.
Drexel University 3250 Chestnut Street, MacAlister Hall, Suite 4020, Philadelphia, PA 19104	GPA: N/A SAT (ERW): 590-680 SAT (M): 590-700 ACT (C): 25-31 ED: No	Admit Rate: 77% Undergrad Enrollment: 14,616 Total Enrollment: 23,589	BS Photography	Portfolio req.
Temple University 1801 N Broad St, Philadelphia, PA 19122	GPA: 3.48 SAT (ERW): N/A* SAT (M): N/A* ACT (C): N/A* *Test-optional ED: No	Overall College Admit Rate: 71% Undergrad Enrollment: 27,306 Total Enrollment: 37,236	BFA Photography BFA Photography with Entrepreneurial Studies	Portfolio req.

School	Avg. GPA, SAT Evidence-Based Reading Writing (ERW), SAT Math (M), and ACT Composite (C) Early Decision (ED): Yes/No	Admission Statistics	Program(s)	Portfolio Required (req.)
University of the Arts 320 S. Broad Street, Philadelphia, PA 19102	GPA: N/A SAT (ERW): N/A* SAT (M): N/A* ACT (C): N/A* *Test-optional ED: No	Overall College Admit Rate: 76% Undergrad Enrollment: 1,380 Total Enrollment: 1,530	BFA Photography	Portfolio req.
Providence College 1 Cunningham Square, Providence, RI 02918	GPA: N/A SAT (ERW): 610-680 SAT (M): 600-680 ACT (C): 27-31 ED: Yes	Admit Rate: 54% Undergrad Enrollment: 4,298 Total Enrollment: 4,821	BA Studio Art, concentration: Photography	Portfolio not req.
Rhode Island School of Design (RISD) 2 College St, Providence, RI 02903	GPA: N/A SAT (ERW): 610-700 SAT (M): 640-770 ACT (C): 27-32 ED: Yes	Admit Rate: 27% Undergrad Enrollment: 1,736 Total Enrollment: 2,227	BFA Photography	Portfolio req.

NORTHEAST

MASSACHUSETTS COLLEGE OF ART & DESIGN (MASSART)

Address: 621 Huntington Ave, Boston, MA 02115
Website: *https://massart.edu/degree-programs/photography-bfa*
Contact: *https://massart.edu/contactus*
Phone: (617) 879-7000
Email: admissions@massart.edu

COST OF ATTENDANCE:

In-State Tuition & Fees: $14,200 | **Additional Expenses:** $19,200
Total: $33,400

New England Resident: $31,800 | **Additional Expenses:** $19,200
Total: $51,000

Out-of-State Tuition & Fees: $39,800 | **Additional Expenses:** $19,200
Total: $59,000

Financial Aid: https://massart.edu/financial-aid

ADDITIONAL INFORMATION:

Available Degree(s)

- BFA Photography

Portfolio Requirement

Portfolios are required for incoming students. Submit 15-20 examples of best and most recent work via the Common App. Applicants must not include artwork that copies another artist's work. Creative writing, screenplays, musical recordings, and theater performances are not allowed either.

Scholarships Offered

All eligible applicants are automatically considered for merit scholarships. To be considered, students need to demonstrate high academic achievement and showcase a strong portfolio. Out-of-state applicants may be eligible for the MassArt Merit Scholarship, the MassArt Transfer Merit Scholarship, or the Trustees Scholarship (covers all tuition and fees, renewable for four years). In-state applicants may be considered for the MassArt Merit Scholarship, the MassArt Transfer Merit Scholarship, and the Senator Paul E. Tsongas Scholarship (covers all tuition and fees for four years).

Special Opportunities

MassArt is located in the heart of Boston's artistic community, allowing students to experience a variety of lectures, exhibitions, and concerts. MassArt also brings on speakers for their Photography Lecture Series every semester.

Notable Alumni

Anastasia Cazabon, Alejandra Carles-Tolra, Qinrui Hua, Nathan Ouellette, and Eduardo L. Rivera

FASHION INSTITUTE OF TECHNOLOGY (FIT)

Address: 227 West 27th Street, New York City, NY 10001
Website: *https://www.fitnyc.edu/academics/academic-divisions/art-and-design/photography/index.php*
Contact: *http://www.fitnyc.edu/about/contact/index.php*
Phone: (212) 217-3760
Email: fitinfo@fitnyc.edu

COST OF ATTENDANCE:

In-State Tuition & Fees: $7,920 | **Additional Expenses:** $18,556
Total: $26,476

Out-of-State Tuition & Fees: $22,242 | **Additional Expenses:** $18,556
Total: $40,798

Financial Aid: https://www.fitnyc.edu/admissions/costs/financial-aid/index.php

ADDITIONAL INFORMATION:

Available Degree(s)

- AAS/BFA Photography and Related Media

Portfolio Requirement

All high school students must first apply to the AAS program. Upon completion of the AAS, students may apply for the BFA program. Portfolios are required for incoming students. Submit materials via SlideRoom.

Scholarships Offered

FIT scholarships are donor scholarships typically gifted to students with high financial need. The average award is $1,100.

Special Opportunities

Photography students learn about lighting, composition, and business practices. Students gain real-life experience in the studio as well as through their projects. Guest lectures and seminars are available every semester. An internship is required to earn the BFA degree.

Notable Alumni

Dana Gallagher, Jeffrey Gamble, Max Hilaire, Leif Huron, Erin Kennedy, Nikki Lee, Frank Maresca, Robert Mendolia, Henrik Olund, Erik Rank, Peter Sakas, Brian Silak, Katie Sokoler, David Wagner, and Nadirah Zakariya

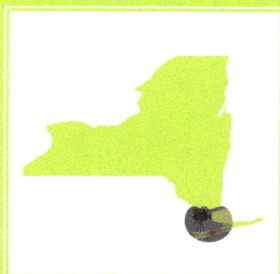

CONNECTICUT

MAINE

MASSACHUSETTS

NEW HAMPSHIRE

NEW JERSEY

NEW YORK

PENNSYLVANIA

RHODE ISLAND

VERMONT

NORTHEAST

CONNECTICUT

MAINE

MASSACHUSETTS

NEW HAMPSHIRE

NEW JERSEY

NEW YORK

PENNSYLVANIA

RHODE ISLAND

VERMONT

NEW YORK UNIVERSITY

Address: 27 West 4th Street, New York, NY 10014
Website: *https://tisch.nyu.edu/photo*
Contact: *https://www.nyu.edu/admissions/undergraduate-admissions/questions.html*
Phone: (212) 998-1900
Email: admissions@nyu.edu

COST OF ATTENDANCE:

Tuition & Fees: $56,500 | **Additional Expenses:** $24,378
Total: $80,878

Financial Aid: https://www.nyu.edu/admissions/financial-aid-and-scholarships.html

ADDITIONAL INFORMATION:

Available Degree(s)

- BFA Photography & Imaging

Portfolio Requirement

Portfolios are required for incoming students. Submit 15-20 images via SlideRoom. At least 10 of the images must follow a single theme. Applicants must also submit short essays and complete a questionnaire.

Scholarships Offered

NYU offers various need-based and/or merit-based scholarships to students in any major. Some examples include the AnBryce Scholarships (GPA 3.5+), the Martin Luther King, Jr., Scholarships, and several others.

Special Opportunities

Photography students explore photo-based imagery through a personal and cultural lens while utilizing 3D simulation technologies, and learning about new media.

Notable Alumni

Zalika Azim, Bryan Denton, Rian Dundon, Monique Jaques, Kieran Kesner, Diane Meyer, Rachel Morrison, Alice Proujansky, Jonno Rattman, Richard Renaldi, and Hank Willis Thomas

PARSONS - THE NEW SCHOOL

Address: 66 Fifth Avenue, New York, NY 10011
Website: *https://www.newschool.edu/parsons/bfa-photography/*
Contact: *https://www.newschool.edu/parsons/contact/*
Phone: (212) 229-8900
Email: thinkparsons@newschool.edu

COST OF ATTENDANCE:

Tuition & Fees: $51,722 | **Additional Expenses:** N/A
Total: $51,722

Financial Aid: https://www.newschool.edu/financial-aid/

ADDITIONAL INFORMATION:

Available Degree(s)

- BFA Photography

Portfolio Requirement

Portfolios are required for incoming students. Applicants must submit 8-12 works in a range of media, however they are encouraged to address the major to which they are applying. All applicants must also submit the Parsons Challenge. This requires that applicants create a new visual work inspired by a theme in your portfolio. A 500-word essay must accompany the new work.

Scholarships Offered

The New School offers merit-based and need-based aid to students. Students are automatically considered for merit-based scholarships. These are based on the strength of the application and portfolio. Need-based aid is available to students who are eligible and submit the FAFSA.

Special Opportunities

The photography program is research-based and studio-intensive. Students explore visual communication and the convergence of documentary, fashion, and artistic themes within photography. Students study installation, 3D imaging, motion capture, and other modalities.

Notable Alumni

Richard Avedon, Erik Madigan Heck, Kevin Kwan, and Steven Meisel

CONNECTICUT

MAINE

MASSACHUSETTS

NEW HAMPSHIRE

NEW JERSEY

NEW YORK

PENNSYLVANIA

RHODE ISLAND

VERMONT

NORTHEAST

CONNECTICUT

MAINE

MASSACHUSETTS

NEW HAMPSHIRE

NEW JERSEY

NEW YORK

PENNSYLVANIA

RHODE ISLAND

VERMONT

PRATT INSTITUTE

Address: 200 Willoughby Avenue, Brooklyn, NY 11205
Website: *https://www.pratt.edu/academics/school-of-art/
undergraduate-school-of-art/photography/photography-bfa/*
Contact: *https://www.pratt.edu/academics/school-of-design/
undergraduate-school-of-design/fashion/fashion-department-
contact/*
Phone: (718) 636-3600
Email: admissions@pratt.edu

COST OF ATTENDANCE:

Tuition & Fees: $53,566 | **Additional Expenses:** $19,824
Total: $73,390

Financial Aid: https://www.pratt.edu/admissions/financing-your-
education/financing-undergraduate/

ADDITIONAL INFORMATION:

Available Degree(s)

- BFA Photography

Portfolio Requirement

Portfolios are required for incoming students. Submit 12-20 works
via SlideRoom. Photography applicants are not required to submit
the 3-5 observational drawings that most other majors must submit,
however they are encouraged to since the first year of study will
entail drawing, painting, and sculpture. There is no writing sample
requirement.

Scholarships Offered

Pratt offers merit-based and endowed scholarships in addition to
need-based grants. Furthermore, there are merit-based scholarships
available to international students as well. The Presidential Merit-
Based Scholarships are available to all Pratt students in varied
award amounts.

Special Opportunities

Pratt hosts the Photography Talk Series, where special guests
give lectures for students. Students may also be interested in
contributing to Pratt's Pounds Per Image/Pratt Photography Imprint
(PPI) publication series. This publication is an annual signature
series.

Notable Alumni

William Gedney, Jan Groover, George Kalinsky, Gertrude Kasebier,
and Sylvia Plachy

ROCHESTER INSTITUTE OF TECHNOLOGY

Address: 209 East 23rd Street, New York, NY 10010
Website: *https://www.rit.edu/study/photographic-and-imaging-arts-bfa*
Contact: *https://www.rit.edu/admissions/contacts*
Phone: (585) 475-6631
Email: admissions@rit.edu

COST OF ATTENDANCE:

Tuition & Fees: $54,058 | **Additional Expenses:** $18,296
Total: $72,354

Financial Aid: https://www.rit.edu/admissions/financial-aid

ADDITIONAL INFORMATION:

Available Degree(s)

- BFA Photographic and Imaging Arts

Portfolio Requirement

Portfolios are not required for first-year applicants.

Scholarships Offered

All applicants are considered for merit-based scholarships upon submission of their application. No separate application is required. RIT also offers numerous merit-based and need-based scholarships for students from different backgrounds or different majors.

Special Opportunities

Photography students may choose an area of concentration in photography, fine art photography, photojournalism, or visual media. The photography major is immersive and involves a hands-on approach to studying the field. RIT also encourages cooperative education and internships, and photography majors earn real-world experience while studying.

Notable Alumni

Kwaku Alston, Paul Benoit, Bernie Boston, Robert F. Bukaty, David Carson, Dean Chamberlain, Bruce Davidson, Pari Dukovic, Ken Geiger, Stan Grossfeld, Tom Hussey, Kenneth Josephson, Dan Loh, Keith Major, Neil Montanus, David Muench, Waalid Raad, Wallace Seawell, William Snyder, David Spindel, Anthony Suau, Pete Turner, Jerry Uelsmann, and Craig Varjabedian

CONNECTICUT

MAINE

MASSACHUSETTS

NEW HAMPSHIRE

NEW JERSEY

NEW YORK

PENNSYLVANIA

RHODE ISLAND

VERMONT

NORTHEAST

CONNECTICUT

MAINE

MASSACHUSETTS

NEW HAMPSHIRE

NEW JERSEY

NEW YORK

PENNSYLVANIA

RHODE ISLAND

VERMONT

SCHOOL OF VISUAL ARTS (SVA)

Address: 209 East 23rd Street, New York, NY 10010
Website: *https://sva.edu/academics/undergraduate/bfa-photography-and-video*
Contact: *https://sva.edu/contact-and-map*
Phone: (212) 592- 2100
Email: admissions@sva.edu

COST OF ATTENDANCE:

Tuition & Fees: $49,750 | **Additional Expenses:** N/A
Total: $49,750

Financial Aid: https://sva.edu/admissions/financial-resources/financial-aid

ADDITIONAL INFORMATION:

Available Degree(s)

- BFA Photography and Video

Portfolio Requirement

Portfolios are required for incoming students. Submit 10-20 photographs or videos via SlideRoom. Portfolios must contain at least 5 photographs. SVA suggests applicants submit work that explores a theme and demonstrates an understanding of light, form, and space.

Scholarships Offered

The Silad H. Rhodes Scholarship is available to students of all majors with an unlisted award amount. Students with a GPA of 3.0+ are eligible. First-time freshmen applicants must submit all application materials by February to be considered. There is no separate application.

Special Opportunities

Photography and Video students learn about analog and digital photography and video. Students also learn how to professionally light a studio, how to shoot, edit, and present video. Furthermore, students may specialize in art, advertising, fashion, portraiture, photojournalism, still-life, landscape, narrative, or a combination of areas.

Notable Alumni

David Attie, Michael Avedon, Alison Brady, David Carol, Renée Cox, Nona Faustine, Ina Jang, Simen Johan, Noah Kalina, Justine Kurland, David LaChapelle, Olivia Locher, Janelle Lynch, Matuschka, Yamini Nayar, Signe Pierce, Lorna Simpson, Amy Stein, Daniel Traub, Shen Wei, and Romulo Yanes

ST. JOHN'S UNIVERSITY

Address: 8000 Utopia Pkwy, Queens, NY 11439
Website: *https://www.stjohns.edu/academics/programs/photography-bachelor-fine-arts*
Contact: *https://www.stjohns.edu/admission/connect-us*
Phone: (718) 990-2000
Email: admhelp@stjohns.edu

COST OF ATTENDANCE:

Tuition & Fees: $46,050 | **Additional Expenses:** $21,208
Total: $67,258

Financial Aid: https://www.stjohns.edu/admission/tuition-and-financial-aid

ADDITIONAL INFORMATION:

Available Degree(s)

- BFA Photography

Portfolio Requirement

Typically, a portfolio is required for admission to the BFA Photography program. However, in the last admissions cycle, St. John's waived this requirement due to COVID-19.

Scholarships Offered

St. John's offers merit-based and need-based scholarships to students. Freshmen who attend the St. John's University Accepted Student Day receive a $250 tuition grant for their first year. Furthermore, all new first-time freshmen who submit their application materials by the first week of December receive a one-time $500 award towards their books. St. John's offers scholarships to up to $3,000 per year for Catholic High School students.

Special Opportunities

The BFA in Photography teaches students technical skills along with the historical foundation of photography within visual arts. Students also have the opportunity to earn ICP certification.

Notable Alumni

Abigail Montes

CONNECTICUT

MAINE

MASSACHUSETTS

NEW HAMPSHIRE

NEW JERSEY

NEW YORK

PENNSYLVANIA

RHODE ISLAND

VERMONT

NORTHEAST

CONNECTICUT

MAINE

MASSACHUSETTS

NEW HAMPSHIRE

NEW JERSEY

NEW YORK

PENNSYLVANIA

RHODE ISLAND

VERMONT

SUNY BUFFALO

Address: 285 Alumni Arena, North Campus, Buffalo, New York 14260
Website: *https://arts-sciences.buffalo.edu/art/research/research-overview/photography.html*
Contact: *https://admissions.buffalo.edu/contact/*
Phone: (716) 645-6900
Email: ub-admissions@buffalo.edu

COST OF ATTENDANCE

In-State Tuition & Fees: $7,270 | **Additional Expenses:** $39,066
Total: $46,336

Out-of-State Tuition & Fees: $24,740.00 | **Additional Expenses:** $4126
Total: $28,866

Financial Aid: https://financialaid.buffalo.edu/

ADDITIONAL INFORMATION:

Available Degree(s)

- BFA Fine Arts, Concentration: Photography

Portfolio Requirement

There is no portfolio requirement.

Scholarships Offered

University at Buffalo offers various merit-based and need-based scholarships and grants including the Presidential Scholarship and the Provost Scholarship.

Special Opportunities

SUNY Buffalo houses a photography lab that includes equipment such as iMacs, various types of printers, scanners, lights, studio lighting, enlargers, tripods, camera kits, darkroom supplies, and more.

Notable Alumni

Ellen Carey, Anne Turyn, and Bil Zelman

SYRACUSE UNIVERSITY

Address: 202 Crouse College, Syracuse, NY 13244
Website: *https://vpa.syr.edu/academics/film-media-arts/programs/art-photo-bfa/*
Contact: *https://www.syracuse.edu/admissions/undergraduate/contact/*
Phone: (315) 443-2769
Email: admissu@syr.edu

COST OF ATTENDANCE:

Tuition & Fees: $57,591 | **Additional Expenses:** $44,448.8
Total: $80,039.80

Financial Aid: https://www.syracuse.edu/admissions/cost-and-aid/

ADDITIONAL INFORMATION:

Available Degree(s)

- BA Photography
- BFA Art Photography

Portfolio Requirement

Portfolios are required for the BFA program. Submit 12-20 photography works and a 300-word response to an essay prompt. Submit all materials via SlideRoom.

Scholarships Offered

Syracuse University offers various merit-based and need-based scholarships and grants. The 1870 Scholarship covers full tuition for the full length of the undergraduate program. Artistic Scholarships are awarded to students based on talent and a maintained cumulative GPA of 2.75+.

Special Opportunities

The BFA in Art Photography dives into cinema, documentary, fashion, contemporary, and ecology in relation to photography. Students build their professional skills and technical skills simultaneously. The program has a partnership with Light Work, a photography center on the Syracuse campus that hosts workshops, lectures, and production facilities. Syracuse also offers a BA in Photography through the Newhouse School of Public Communications

Notable Alumni

Nydia Blas, Joe McNally, John Pfahl, and Stephanie Welsh

CONNECTICUT

MAINE

MASSACHUSETTS

NEW HAMPSHIRE

NEW JERSEY

NEW YORK

PENNSYLVANIA

RHODE ISLAND

VERMONT

NORTHEAST

CONNECTICUT

MAINE

MASSACHUSETTS

NEW HAMPSHIRE

NEW JERSEY

NEW YORK

PENNSYLVANIA

RHODE ISLAND

VERMONT

DREXEL UNIVERSITY

Address: 3141 Chestnut Street, Philadelphia, PA 19104
Website: *https://drexel.edu/westphal/academics/undergraduate/PHTO/*
Contact: *https://drexel.edu/westphal/about/contact/*
Phone: (215) 895-2000
Email: westphal.admissions@drexel.edu

COST OF ATTENDANCE:

Tuition & Fees: $57,171 | **Additional Expenses:** $19,388
Total: $76,559

Financial Aid: https://drexel.edu/drexelcentral/finaid/overview/

ADDITIONAL INFORMATION:

Available Degree(s)

- BS Photography

Portfolio Requirement

Portfolios are required for incoming students. Submit 8-12 of your strongest works in a variety of media that showcases a balance of technique and concept. Submit via SlideRoom.

Scholarships Offered

Westphal Portfolio Scholarship available to incoming first-year students based on outstanding portfolio work. Amount awarded is not listed. In addition, merit-based awards and other scholarships are available.

Special Opportunities

Drexel hosts the annual High School Photography Contest. Furthermore, their photography program has produced graduates who have won the Pulitzer Prize for Photojournalism, The Guggenheim Fellowship, and a feature at the AIPAD. Photography students learn various technical skills in the darkroom, digitally, and how to incorporate motion. They also are required to have a six-month co-op in the industry along with three business courses.

Notable Alumni

Mattison Becker, Hannah Beier, Tyler Haughey, Kelsey Fain, Peter Kubilus, Samuel Markey, Harris Mizrahi, Alexa Nahas, Jane Greer Raese, Andre Rucker, Jeffrey Stockbridge, and Jason Varney

TEMPLE UNIVERSITY

Address: 1801 N Broad St, Philadelphia, PA 19122
Website: *https://tyler.temple.edu/programs/photography*
Contact: *https://www.temple.edu/contact/*
Phone: (215) 204-7000
Email: askanowl@temple.edu

COST OF ATTENDANCE:

In-State Tuition & Fees: $18,168 | **Additional Expenses:** $17,880
Total: $36,048

Out-of-State Tuition & Fees: $31,440 | **Additional Expenses:** $19,944
Total: $51,384

Financial Aid: https://admissions.temple.edu/costs-aid-scholarships/financial-aid-scholarships

ADDITIONAL INFORMATION:

Available Degree(s)

- BFA Photography
- BFA Photography with Entrepreneurial Studies

Portfolio Requirement

Portfolios are required for incoming students. Submit up to 20 works via Slideroom.

Scholarships Offered

All students who submit their application by February 1 are automatically considered for merit scholarships. Award amounts range from $1,000 to full tuition.

Special Opportunities

Temple University was the first college to offer coursework in color photography. The BFA in Photography emphasizes a historical perspective and allows students to learn about alternative techniques such as hand-applied emulsions, platinum printing, gum printing, and more.

Notable Alumni

Hazziza Abdullah, Bill Davis, Vincent Feldman, David Graham, Matt Haffner, Gabriel Martinez, Rachelle Mozman, Nicholas Muellner, Laurie Simmons, Ivette Spradlin, and Jessica Parris Westbrook

CONNECTICUT

MAINE

MASSACHUSETTS

NEW HAMPSHIRE

NEW JERSEY

NEW YORK

PENNSYLVANIA

RHODE ISLAND

VERMONT

NORTHEAST

CONNECTICUT

MAINE

MASSACHUSETTS

NEW HAMPSHIRE

NEW JERSEY

NEW YORK

PENNSYLVANIA

RHODE ISLAND

VERMONT

UNIVERSITY OF THE ARTS

Address: 320 S. Broad Street, Philadelphia, PA 19102
Website: *https://www.uarts.edu/academics/photography*
Contact: *https://www.uarts.edu/about/contact-us*
Phone: (215) 717-6049
Email: admissions@uarts.edu

COST OF ATTENDANCE:

Tuition & Fees: $48,350 | **Additional Expenses:** $20,600
Total: $68,950

Financial Aid: https://www.uarts.edu/tuition-and-financial-aid

ADDITIONAL INFORMATION:

Available Degree(s)

- BFA Photography

Portfolio Requirement

Scholarships Offered

Various named scholarships are available to all students for varied award amounts. Some scholarships are available to all University of the Arts students, such as the W.W. Smith Scholarship, the James M. Cresson, Scholarship, the Arnold A. Bayard Scholarship, and more.

Special Opportunities

Photography students have access to state-of-the-art facilities such as newly renovated imaging labs, a laptop lab, studio lighting classrooms, new printers, a photo finishing room, and more.

Notable Alumni

Takashi Aoyama, Marcus Branch, Hannah Bohrer, Cathay Edelman, Dominic Episcopo, Hannah Fielo, James Izlar, David Lebe, Jessica Lim, Molly Smith, Jamie Stow, Rebecca Torres, German Ayala Vazquez, Georgia Westcott, Destiny Williams, and Deborah Willis

PROVIDENCE COLLEGE

Address: 1 Cunningham Square, Providence, RI 02918
Website: *https://art.providence.edu/studio-art/photography/*
Contact: *https://admission.providence.edu/contact/*
Phone: (401) 865-1000
Email: pcadmiss@providence.edu

COST OF ATTENDANCE:

Tuition & Fees: $55,850 | **Additional Expenses:** $18,522
Total: $74,372

Financial Aid: https://financial-aid.providence.edu/

ADDITIONAL INFORMATION:

Available Degree(s)

- BA Studio Art, concentration: Photography

Portfolio Requirement

Portfolios are not required for incoming students.

Scholarships Offered

Providence College offers merit-based tuition scholarships ranging from $20,000 to $35,000 per year. No separate application is required. Students are evaluated based on their application. Furthermore, Providence College offers the Fine Arts Tuition Scholarship, which judges students based on their portfolio work.

Special Opportunities

Students undergo an annual faculty critique where they showcase their year of work and gain feedback from a panel of professors. Photography students also complete a capstone project and cultivate a strong portfolio for preparation when applying for jobs post-graduation.

Notable Alumni

Stephan Brigidi, Samantha Cataldo, Stephen Forneris, Helena Gomez, Will Hutnick, Hannah Johnson, Mark Mazzenga, Molly O'Brien, Hendrick Paul, Mary Pelletier, Maura Reilly, Michael Rose, William Ruggiero, Althea Ruoppo, Eric Schofield, and Mary Tinti

CONNECTICUT

MAINE

MASSACHUSETTS

NEW HAMPSHIRE

NEW JERSEY

NEW YORK

PENNSYLVANIA

RHODE ISLAND

VERMONT

NORTHEAST

CONNECTICUT

MAINE

MASSACHUSETTS

NEW HAMPSHIRE

NEW JERSEY

NEW YORK

PENNSYLVANIA

RHODE ISLAND

VERMONT

RHODE ISLAND SCHOOL OF DESIGN (RISD)

Address: 2 College St, Providence, RI 02903
Website: *https://www.risd.edu/academics/photography/bachelors-program*
Contact: *https://www.risd.edu/academics/apparel-design/contact/*
Phone: (401) 454-6300
Email: admissions@risd.edu

COST OF ATTENDANCE:

Tuition & Fees: $55,220 | **Additional Expenses:** $22,060
Total: $77,280

Financial Aid: https://www.risd.edu/student-financial-services/undergraduate-aid/

ADDITIONAL INFORMATION:

Available Degree(s)

- BFA Photography

Portfolio Requirement

Portfolios are required for incoming students. Submit 12-20 works to SlideRoom. RISD strongly encourages including works that involve drawing from direct observation.

Scholarships Offered

RISD scholarships are need-based. Students must submit a FAFSA application each year to be considered. RISD is also partnered with Scholarship Universe, a website that matches students with outside scholarships and keeps students on track with deadlines.

Special Opportunities

The photography cohort has approximately 30 undergraduates that work closely with the approximately 15 graduate students. BFA and MFA students share some darkrooms and workspaces. Students participate in critiques, informal discussions, and numerous exhibitions at the department's Red Eye Gallery.

Notable Alumni

Matthew Barbarino, Darby Clarke, Ashley Hagerstrand, Travis Morehead, John Shen, Mélissa St-Pierre, Yixuan Wu, and Hantian Xue

ILLINOIS

INDIANA

IOWA

KANSAS

MICHIGAN

MINNESOTA

MISSOURI

NEBRASKA

NORTH DAKOTA

OHIO

SOUTH DAKOTA

WISCONSIN

CHAPTER 12

REGION TWO

MIDWEST

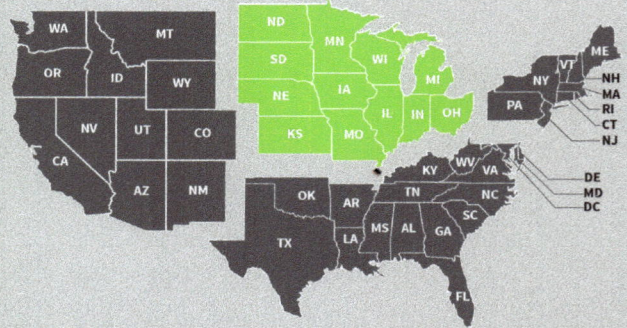

11 *Programs* | 12 *States*

1. IL – Columbia College Chicago
2. IL - School of the Art Institute Chicago
3. IL - University of Illinois, Urbana-Champaign
4. IN - Purdue University
5. IA - University of Iowa
6. MO - Washington University, St. Louis
7. OH - Cleveland Institute of Art
8. OH - Columbus College of Art & Design
9. OH - Kent State University
10. OH - Ohio University
11. OH - University of Dayton

PHOTOGRAPHY PROGRAMS

School	Avg. GPA, SAT Evidence-Based Reading Writing (ERW), SAT Math (M), and ACT Composite (C) Early Decision (ED): Yes/No	Admission Statistics	Program(s)	Portfolio Required (req.)
Columbia College Chicago 600 S Michigan Ave, Chicago, IL 60605	GPA: N/A SAT (ERW): N/A* SAT (M): N/A* ACT (C): N/A* *Test-optional ED: Yes	Overall College Admit Rate: 90% Undergrad Enrollment: 6,542 Total Enrollment: 6,769	BA Photography BFA Photography	BFA: Portfolio req. BA: Portfolio optional
School of the Art Institute of Chicago (SAIC) 36 S. Wabash Ave., Chicago, IL 60603	GPA: N/A SAT (ERW): 560-660 SAT (M): 480-600 ACT (C): 22-25 ED: No	Admit Rate: 78% Undergrad Enrollment: 2,487 Total Enrollment: 3,132	BFA Photography	Portfolio req.
University of Illinois Urbana-Champaign (UIUC) 901 West Illinois Street, Urbana, IL 61801	GPA: N/A SAT (ERW): 590-700 SAT (M): 620-770 ACT (C): 27-33 ED: Yes	Overall College Admit Rate: 50% Undergrad Enrollment: 34,559 Total Enrollment: 56,257	BA Studio Art: Photography BFA Studio Art: Photography	Portfolio req.
Purdue University Purdue University, West Lafayette, IN 47907	GPA: 3.67 SAT (ERW): 590-690 SAT (M): 600-740 ACT (C): 25-33 ED: No	Overall College Admit Rate: 67% Undergrad Enrollment: 34,920 Total Enrollment: 45,869	BFA Integrated Studio Arts: Art, Culture, & Technology	Portfolio req.

School	Avg. GPA, SAT Evidence-Based Reading Writing (ERW), SAT Math (M), and ACT Composite (C) Early Decision (ED): Yes/No	Admission Statistics	Program(s)	Portfolio Required (req.)
University of Iowa University of Iowa, Iowa City, IA 52242	GPA: 3.81 SAT (ERW): 570-680 SAT (M): 560-670 ACT (C): 22-29 ED: No	Overall College Admit Rate: 86% Undergrad Enrollment: 21,608 Total Enrollment: 29,909	BA Studio Art BFA Studio Art: Media, Social Practice & Design	Portfolio not req.
Washington University in St. Louis 1 Brookings Dr, St. Louis, MO 63130	GPA: 4.21 SAT (ERW): 720-760 SAT (M): 760-800 ACT (C): 33-35 ED: Yes	Overall College Admit Rate: 16% Undergrad Enrollment: 7,653 Total Enrollment: 15,449	BFA Studio Art, concentration: Photography	Portfolio req.
Cleveland Institute of Art 11610 Euclid Avenue, Cleveland, OH 44106	GPA: N/A SAT (ERW): 560-680 SAT (M): 510-620 ACT (C): 19-27 ED: No	Overall College Admit Rate: 67% Undergrad Enrollment: 599 Total Enrollment: 599	BFA Photography	Portfolio req.
Columbus College of Art and Design 60 Cleveland Ave, Columbus, OH 43215	GPA: N/A SAT (ERW): N/A SAT (M): N/A ACT (C): N/A *Test-optional ED: No	Admit Rate: 92% Undergrad Enrollment: 982 Total Enrollment: 1,009	BFA Photography	Portfolio req.

MIDWEST

PHOTOGRAPHY PROGRAMS

School	Avg. GPA, SAT Evidence-Based Reading Writing (ERW), SAT Math (M), and ACT Composite (C) Early Decision (ED): Yes/No	Admission Statistics	Program(s)	Portfolio Required (req.)
Kent State University 1325 Theatre Drive, Kent, OH 44242	GPA: 3.61 SAT (ERW): 510-610 SAT (M): 510-600 ACT (C): 20-26 ED: No	Overall College Admit Rate: 84% Undergrad Enrollment: 21,621 Total Enrollment: 26,822	BFA Photography	Portfolio not req.
Ohio University Ohio University, Athens, OH 45701	GPA: 3.55 SAT (ERW): 530-630 SAT (M): 520-620 ACT (C): 21-26 ED: No	Overall College Admit Rate: 87% Undergrad Enrollment: 19,284 Total Enrollment: 25,714	BFA Studio Art, concentration: Photography & Integrated Media	Portfolio req.
University of Dayton 300 College Park, Dayton, OH 45469	GPA: 3.73 SAT (ERW): 540-640 SAT (M): 540-660 ACT (C): 23-29 ED: No	Overall College Admit Rate: 81% Undergrad Enrollment:8,644 Total Enrollment: 11,650	BFA Photography	Portfolio not req.

COLUMBIA COLLEGE CHICAGO

Address: 600 S. Michigan Avenue, Chicago, IL 60605
Website: *https://www.colum.edu/academics/programs/photography-ba*
Contact: *https://www.colum.edu/contact*
Phone: (312) 369-1000
Email: admissions@colum.edu

COST OF ATTENDANCE:

Tuition & Fees: $35,716 | **Additional Expenses:** $18,000
Total: $53,716

Financial Aid: https://www.colum.edu/columbia-central/where-to-start/index

ADDITIONAL INFORMATION:

Available Degree(s)
- BA Photography
- BFA Photography

Portfolio Requirement

Portfolios are required for entry to the BFA program. They are optional for the BA program, however strongly encouraged, as a portfolio is required to be considered for the Faculty Recognition Award. Submit 10 photographs taken within the last year and pass an online photography exam.

Scholarships Offered

Students are automatically considered for renewable scholarships upon admission. For need-based scholarship, submit a FAFSA. For talent-based scholarships, submit an audition that demonstrates your best creative work. First-year, international students may be considered for talent-based scholarships.

Special Opportunities

Columbia College Chicago offers three concentrations for photography majors: Commercial Photography; Fine Art Photography; and Fashion Photography. From the first course, students jump straight into photography experimentation and experiential learning opportunities. Furthermore, most photography students pursue 1+ internships during their junior and senior year.

Notable Alumni

Matt Austin, Greg Harris, Katie Levine, Ryan Lowry, Hannah Soto, Alex Wieder, and Martha Williams

ILLINOIS

INDIANA

IOWA

KANSAS

MICHIGAN

MINNESOTA

MISSOURI

NEBRASKA

NORTH DAKOTA

OHIO

SOUTH DAKOTA

WISCONSIN

SCHOOL OF THE ART INSTITUTE OF CHICAGO (SAIC)

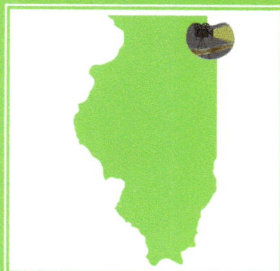

Address: 36 S. Wabash Ave., Chicago, IL 60603
Website: *https://www.saic.edu/academics/departments/ photography/undergraduate-overview*
Contact: *https://www.saic.edu/contact/*
Phone: (312) 629-6101
Email: admiss@saic.edu

COST OF ATTENDANCE:

Tuition & Fees: $53,360 | **Additional Expenses:** $21,200
Total: $74,560

Financial Aid: https://www.saic.edu/financial-aid/

ADDITIONAL INFORMATION:

Available Degree(s)

- BFA Photography

Portfolio Requirement

Portfolios are required for incoming students. Submit 10-15 works and showcase a breadth of media.

Scholarships Offered

SAIC offers Presidential, Distinguished, Honors, Recognition, Incentive, and Enrichment scholarships at varied amounts. These merit scholarships are based on the student's portfolio and application materials. In addition, students who participated in certain art exhibitions or competitions may be eligible for the Competitive Excellence Award ($2000).

Need-based scholarships are also available. Some of these include the John and Mary E. Hoggins Scholarship for female SAIC students, the Roger Brown and George Veronda Scholarship, or the LeRoy Neiman Scholarship. Award amounts vary.

Special Opportunities

Students collaborate with graduate students to create the annual departmental catalog. Furthermore, students may participate in a credit-earning Senior Seminar focused on professional development. This seminar is the capstone class for BFA students.

Notable Alumni

Natalie Bookchin, Joyce Neimanas, Darryl DeAngelo Terrell, and William Vandivert

ILLINOIS

INDIANA

IOWA

KANSAS

MICHIGAN

MINNESOTA

MISSOURI

NEBRASKA

NORTH DAKOTA

OHIO

SOUTH DAKOTA

WISCONSIN

MIDWEST

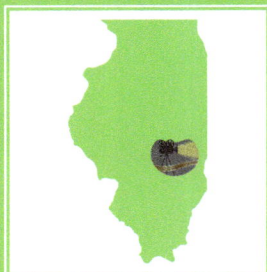

ILLINOIS

INDIANA

IOWA

KANSAS

MICHIGAN

MINNESOTA

MISSOURI

NEBRASKA

NORTH DAKOTA

OHIO

SOUTH DAKOTA

WISCONSIN

UNIVERSITY OF ILLINOIS URBANA-CHAMPAIGN (UIUC)

Address: 901 West Illinois Street, Urbana, IL 61801
Website: *https://art.illinois.edu/programs-and-applying/bachelors-programs/studio-art-ba-bfa/photography/*
Contact: *https://admissions.illinois.edu/contact*
Phone: (217) 333-0302
Email: admissions@illinois.edu

COST OF ATTENDANCE:

In-State Tuition & Fees: $16,866 | **Additional Expenses:** $16,194
Total: $33,060

Out-of-State Tuition & Fees: $34,316 | **Additional Expenses:** $16,534
Total: $50,850

Financial Aid: https://admissions.illinois.edu/Invest/financial-aid

ADDITIONAL INFORMATION:

Available Degree(s)

- BA Studio Art: Photography
- BFA Studio Art: Photography

Portfolio Requirement

Portfolios are required for incoming students. Submit 10 recent works showcasing a breadth of media, and an optional 2 direct video links or a web address that links to your portfolio. Drawings from observation and preferred.

Scholarships Offered

Both in-state and out-of-state applicants are eligible for various merit-based and need-based scholarships.

Special Opportunities

The photography program at UIUC provides a balanced approach to photography, where students learn about research, history, and the integration of creativity along with the necessary technical skills. Students have access to Mac and Windows workstations, darkrooms, scanners, printers, cameras, editing facilities, shooting studios, and more.

Notable Alumni

Eli Craven, Kendall Hill, and Brittany Pyle

PURDUE UNIVERSITY

Address: Purdue University, West Lafayette, IN 47907
Website: *https://cla.purdue.edu/academic/rueffschool/ad/isa/p_ArtCultTech_Overview.html*
Contact: *https://www.admissions.purdue.edu/contact/index.php*
Phone: (765) 494-4600
Email: admissions@purdue.edu

COST OF ATTENDANCE:

In-State Tuition & Fees: $10,052 | **Additional Expenses:** $12,820
Total: $22,872

Out-of-State Tuition & Fees: $28,854 | **Additional Expenses:** $12,820
Total: $41,674

Financial Aid: https://www.purdue.edu/dfa/

ADDITIONAL INFORMATION:

Available Degree(s)

* BFA Integrated Studio Arts: Art, Culture, & Technology

Portfolio Requirement

Portfolios are required for incoming students.

Scholarships Offered

Purdue awards freshman scholarships based on academic merit as well as financial need. The Trustees Scholarship awards $10,000 per year to in-state students and $16,000 per year to out-of-state students. The Presidential Scholarship awards $4,000 per year to in-state students and $10,000 per year to out-of-state students.

Special Opportunities

This relatively new program brings an interdisciplinary approach to the BFA. In the Art, Culture, and Technology concentration, students study photography, video, physical computing, and new media culture. Students may choose to further specialize in an area of study: Electronic & Time-Based Art or Photography and Related Media.

Notable Alumni

Gary Mark Smith

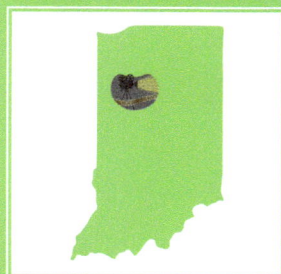

ILLINOIS

INDIANA

IOWA

KANSAS

MICHIGAN

MINNESOTA

MISSOURI

NEBRASKA

NORTH DAKOTA

OHIO

SOUTH DAKOTA

WISCONSIN

MIDWEST

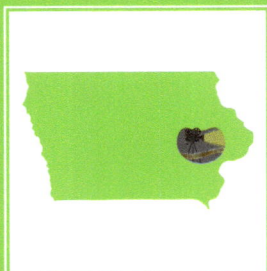

UNIVERSITY OF IOWA

Address: University of Iowa, Iowa City, IA 52242
Website: *https://art.uiowa.edu/areas/photography*
Contact: *https://admissions.uiowa.edu/contact-us*
Phone: (319) 335-3847
Email: admissions@uiowa.edu

COST OF ATTENDANCE:

In-State Tuition & Fees: $9,942 | **Additional Expenses:** $16,530
Total: $26,472

Out-of-State Tuition & Fees: $31,905 | **Additional Expenses:** $16,530
Total: $48,435

Financial Aid: https://admissions.uiowa.edu/finances

ADDITIONAL INFORMATION:

Available Degree(s)

- BA Studio Art
- BFA Studio Art: Media, Social Practice & Design

Portfolio Requirement

There is no portfolio requirement for incoming students.

Scholarships Offered

The University of Iowa offers merit-based and need-based scholarships to all students. Students are automatically considered for merit scholarships upon submitting their university application. Students are also encouraged to apply to externally-funded scholarships.

Special Opportunities

The BFA in Studio Art: Media, Social Practice, & Design has students learning about graphic design, intermedia, and photography. Meanwhile, the BA is in Studio Art and students learn about photography through their coursework.

The University of Iowa offers state-of-the-art facilities such as an 8-station darkroom, various printers, brand new scanners and portable strobe kits, and more. Furthermore, this interdisciplinary program encourages exploration across disciplines and photography students are welcome to experiment with 3D printing, laser and plasma cutters, and other tools.

Notable Alumni

Kyle Agnew, Aspen DeRosa, Taylor Hedrick, Annie Hodgkins, Colin Murray, Barry Phipps, and Hao Zhou

ILLINOIS

INDIANA

IOWA

KANSAS

MICHIGAN

MINNESOTA

MISSOURI

NEBRASKA

NORTH DAKOTA

OHIO

SOUTH DAKOTA

WISCONSIN

WASHINGTON UNIVERSITY IN ST. LOUIS

Address: 1 Brookings Dr., St. Louis, MO 63130
Website: *https://samfoxschool.wustl.edu/academics/college-of-art/bfa-ba-in-studio-art-and-design/studio-art*
Contact: *https://admissions.wustl.edu/contact-us/*
Phone: (314) 935-5858
Email: admissions@wustl.edu

COST OF ATTENDANCE:

Tuition & Fees: $57,750 | **Additional Expenses:** $19,016
Total: $76,766

Financial Aid: https://financialaid.wustl.edu/

ADDITIONAL INFORMATION:

Available Degree(s)

- BFA Studio Art, concentration: Photography

Portfolio Requirement

Portfolios are required for incoming students. Submit 10-20 works.

Scholarships Offered

WashU offers merit-based and need-based scholarships for students in any major. Some of these institutional scholarships cover the full cost of tuition. They also offer the Signature Scholar Program, which involves individual applications and a weekend program. Partial and full tuition are offered within this scholarship program.

Special Opportunities

Approximately half of the studio art student's coursework is in creating real-life pieces in the studio. Other concentrations include painting, printmaking, sculpture, or time-based and media art. Students are required to complete a capstone and participate in the annual thesis exhibition.

Notable Alumni

Brian Cui, Jiyoon Kang, and Benjamin Levine

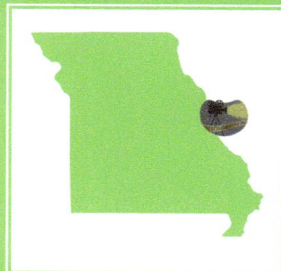

ILLINOIS

INDIANA

IOWA

KANSAS

MICHIGAN

MINNESOTA

MISSOURI

NEBRASKA

NORTH DAKOTA

OHIO

SOUTH DAKOTA

WISCONSIN

MIDWEST

ILLINOIS

INDIANA

IOWA

KANSAS

MICHIGAN

MINNESOTA

MISSOURI

NEBRASKA

NORTH DAKOTA

OHIO

SOUTH DAKOTA

WISCONSIN

CLEVELAND INSTITUTE OF ART

Address: 11610 Euclid Avenue, Cleveland, OH 44106
Website: *https://www.cia.edu/academics/photography*
Contact: *https://www.cia.edu/contact*
Phone: (216) 421-7000
Email: admissions@cia.edu

COST OF ATTENDANCE:

Tuition & Fees: $45,495 | **Additional Expenses:** $17,010
Total: $62,505

Financial Aid: https://www.cia.edu/admissions/financing-your-education

ADDITIONAL INFORMATION:

Available Degree(s)

- BFA Photography

Portfolio Requirement

Portfolios are required for incoming students. Submit 12-20 works. Sketchbook pages are highly encouraged.

Scholarships Offered

CIA offers renewable merit scholarships to undergraduate students. Students are automatically considered upon acceptance. Students who do not receive a merit scholarship may still be considered for a need-based CIA grant if they submit a FAFSA.

Special Opportunities

Students in the photography program explore specialized lighting techniques, alternative print media, and presentation techniques for publication. CIA is also committed to giving students the opportunity to gain real experience by working with clients or within the public sphere through their Engaged Practice promise.

Notable Alumni

Amy Goldberg and Chris Jungjohann

COLUMBUS COLLEGE OF ART AND DESIGN

Address: 60 Cleveland Ave, Columbus, OH 43215
Website: *https://www.ccad.edu/academics/photography*
Contact: *https://www.ccad.edu/directory*
Phone: (614) 224-9101
Email: admissions@ccad.edu

COST OF ATTENDANCE:

Tuition & Fees: $37,370 | **Additional Expenses:** $17,208
Total: $54,578

Financial Aid: https://www.ccad.edu/admissions/financial-aid

ADDITIONAL INFORMATION:

Available Degree(s)

- BFA Photography

Portfolio Requirement

Portfolios are required for incoming students. Submit 8-15 works.

Scholarships Offered

CCAD offers academic and merit scholarships. There are also external scholarship opportunities, such as the Ohio Governor's Youth Art Exhibition, the Lounge Lizard scholarship competition, MVP Scholarships ($500) and more.

Special Opportunities

Photography students develop their technical skills while also learning how to present their work to clients, alternative processes to developing images, and research. Students have access to a 2,000-square-foot commercial photo studio, a black-and-white darkroom, and an individual photosensitive lab.

Notable Alumni

James Dupree, Inka Essenhigh, Alex Grey, Kerry G. Johnson, Robert McCall, John Jude Palencar, Dan Scanlon, and Timothy Truman

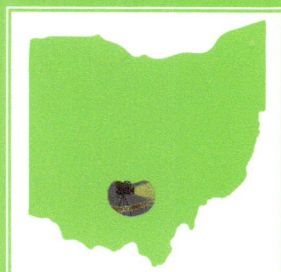

ILLINOIS

INDIANA

IOWA

KANSAS

MICHIGAN

MINNESOTA

MISSOURI

NEBRASKA

NORTH DAKOTA

OHIO

SOUTH DAKOTA

WISCONSIN

MIDWEST

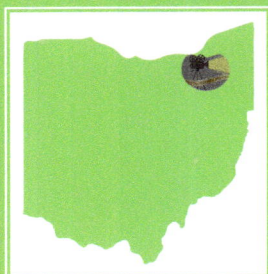

KENT STATE UNIVERSITY

Address: 1325 Theatre Drive, Kent, OH 44242
Website: *https://www.kent.edu/vcd/bachelor-fine-arts-photography*
Contact: *https://www.kent.edu/admissions/contact-us*
Phone: (330) 672-2082
Email: admissions@kent.edu

COST OF ATTENDANCE:

In-State Tuition & Fees: $11,923 | **Additional Expenses:** $17,745
Total: $29,668

Out-of-State Tuition & Fees: $20,799 | **Additional Expenses:** $17,745
Total: $38,544

Financial Aid: https://www.kent.edu/financialaid

ADDITIONAL INFORMATION:

Available Degree(s)

- BFA Photography

Portfolio Requirement

There is no portfolio requirement for incoming students.

Scholarships Offered

Out-of-state students may be eligible for merit-based awards, including the President's Achievement Award ($4,000-$12,500), the Honors Distinction Award ($1,000-$3,000), the Founders Scholarship ($1,000-$2,000) among others. In-state students may be eligible for the same scholarships.

Special Opportunities

In the first two years of study, photography students build technical foundations and learn about studio lighting, the history of photography, rules of composition, and command of the camera. A Sophomore Portfolio review occurs with the portfolio work built in the first two years. At the review, the panel and the student discuss possible career paths and courses of study to focus on.

Notable Alumni

Jermaine Jackson Jr.

ILLINOIS

INDIANA

IOWA

KANSAS

MICHIGAN

MINNESOTA

MISSOURI

NEBRASKA

NORTH DAKOTA

OHIO

SOUTH DAKOTA

WISCONSIN

OHIO UNIVERSITY

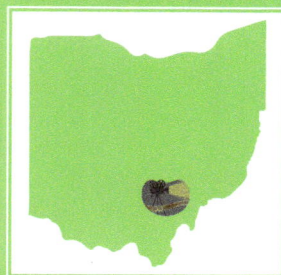

Address: Ohio University, Athens, OH 45701
Website: *https://www.ohio.edu/fine-arts/art/undergraduate/bfa-studio-art/photography-integrated-media*
Contact: *https://www.ohio.edu/admissions/*
Phone: (740) 593-4818
Email: admissions@ohio.edu

COST OF ATTENDANCE:

In-State Tuition & Fees: $12,840 | **Additional Expenses:** $11,862
Total: $24,702

Out-of-State Tuition & Fees: $22,810 | **Additional Expenses:** $11,862
Total: $34,672

Financial Aid: https://www.ohio.edu/admissions/tuition/scholarships-financial-aid

ADDITIONAL INFORMATION:

Available Degree(s)

- BFA Studio Art, concentration: Photography & Integrated Media

Portfolio Requirement

Portfolios are required for incoming students. Submit your 10 best works.

Scholarships Offered

Students who submit their application by the Early Action deadline are automatically considered for the OHIO Excellence Awards. Award amounts vary. There is no separate application required.

Special Opportunities

In 1948, the renowned Clarence White School of Photography in New York was re-established at Ohio University. Photography students gain an understanding of technical processes such as black-and-white photography, digital imaging, and interdisciplinary practice.

Notable Alumni

Ruth-Marion Baruch, Karen T. Borchers, Paul Fusco, Daniel King, Herman Leonard, I.C. Rapoport, Martha Rial, Chuck Stewart, and Kō Yamada

ILLINOIS

INDIANA

IOWA

KANSAS

MICHIGAN

MINNESOTA

MISSOURI

NEBRASKA

NORTH DAKOTA

OHIO

SOUTH DAKOTA

WISCONSIN

MIDWEST

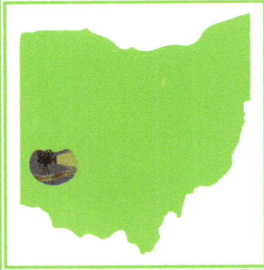

ILLINOIS

INDIANA

IOWA

KANSAS

MICHIGAN

MINNESOTA

MISSOURI

NEBRASKA

NORTH DAKOTA

OHIO

SOUTH DAKOTA

WISCONSIN

UNIVERSITY OF DAYTON

Address: 300 College Park, Dayton, OH 45469
Website: *https://udayton.edu/artssciences/academics/ artanddesign/academic/photography/index.php*
Contact: *https://udayton.edu/apply/contact-admission.php*
Phone: (800) 837-7433
Email: admission@udayton.edu

COST OF ATTENDANCE:

Tuition & Fees: $44,890 | **Additional Expenses:** $14,870
Total: $59,760

Financial Aid: https://udayton.edu/affordability/undergraduate/ financial-aid/index.php

ADDITIONAL INFORMATION:

Available Degree(s)

- BFA Photography

Portfolio Requirement

There is no portfolio for incoming students.

Scholarships Offered

Students are automatically considered for merit scholarships upon submission of their application. No separate application is required. Scholarships range from $16,250 to $31,000 per year for four years.

Special Opportunities

According to the University of Dayton, 100% of their photography students produce a portfolio by graduation and 100% engage in an internship or other experiential learning opportunity prior to graduation.

Notable Alumni

Anthony Grant, Jon Gruden, Jon A. Husted, Kristina Keneally, Brian Roberts, Richard Rohr, Mike Turner, and Nan Whaley

ALABAMA

ARKANSAS

DELAWARE

DISTRICT OF
COLUMBIA

FLORIDA

GEORGIA

KENTUCKY

LOUISIANA

MARYLAND

MISSISSIPPI

NORTH CAROLINA

OKLAHOMA

SOUTH CAROLINA

TENNESSEE

TEXAS

VIRGINIA

WEST VIRGINIA

CHAPTER 13

REGION THREE

SOUTH

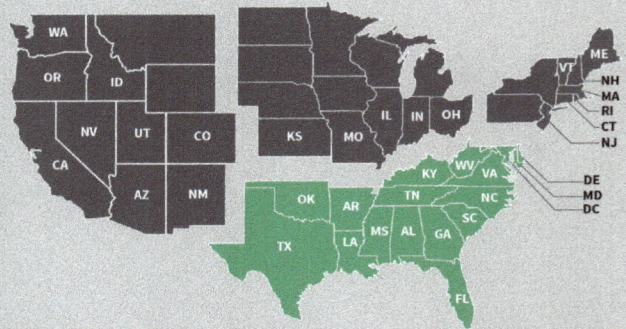

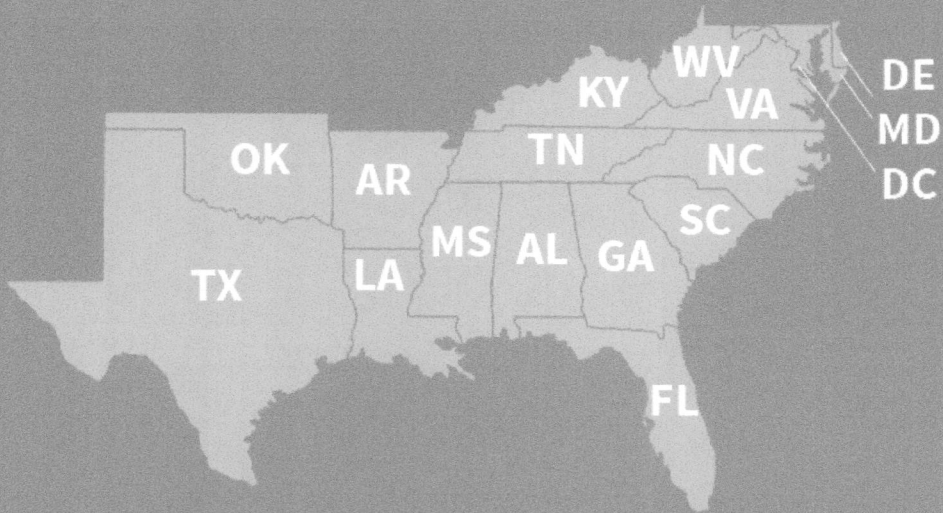

13 Programs | 16 States

1. DC - The George Washington University
2. FL - University of Central Florida
3. FL – University of Miami
4. GA - Savannah College of Art and Design (SCAD)
5. KY - Western Kentucky University
6. LA - Louisiana Tech University
7. MD - Maryland Institute College of Art
8. OK - University of Central Oklahoma
9. TX - Sam Houston State University
10. TX - Texas Christian University
11. TX - Texas State University
12. TX - University of Houston
13. VA - Virginia Commonwealth University

PHOTOGRAPHY PROGRAMS

School	Avg. GPA, SAT Evidence-Based Reading Writing (ERW), SAT Math (M), and ACT Composite (C) Early Decision (ED): Yes/No	Admission Statistics	Program(s)	Portfolio Required (req.)
The George Washington University (GWU) 814 20th Street NW, 3rd Floor, Washington, DC 20052	GPA: N/A SAT (ERW): 640-720 SAT (M): 630-730 ACT (C): 29-33 ED: Yes	Overall College Admit Rate: 43% Undergrad Enrollment: 11,762 Total Enrollment: 27,017	BFA Photojournalism BA Fine Arts, concentration: Photojournalism	BFA: Portfolio req. BA: Portfolio not req.
University of Central Florida 4000 Central Florida Blvd, Orlando, FL 32816	GPA: 4.16 SAT (ERW): 600-680 SAT (M): 570-670 ACT (C): 25-30 ED: No	Overall College Admit Rate: 36% Undergrad Enrollment: 60,075 Total Enrollment: 70,406	BA Art: Studio, Specialization: Photography BFA Studio Art, Specialization: Photography	Portfolio not req.
University of Miami University of Miami, Coral Gables, FL 33124	GPA: 3.6 SAT (ERW): 620-700 SAT (M): 630-720 ACT (C): 28-32 ED: Yes	Overall College Admit Rate: 33% Undergrad Enrollment: 11,334 Total Enrollment: 17,809	BA Art, specialization: Photography BA Studio Art, specialization: Photography BFA Art, specialization: Photography	Portfolio not req.
Savannah College of Art & Design (SCAD) 342 Bull St., Savannah, GA 31401	GPA: 3.6 SAT (ERW): 540-640 SAT (M): 500-600 ACT (C): 20-27 ED: No	Admit Rate: 78% Undergrad Enrollment: 11,679 Total Enrollment: 14,265	BA Photography BFA Photography	Portfolio req.

School	Avg. GPA, SAT Evidence-Based Reading Writing (ERW), SAT Math (M), and ACT Composite (C) Early Decision (ED): Yes/No	Admission Statistics	Program(s)	Portfolio Required (req.)
Western Kentucky University 1906 College Heights Blvd, Bowling Green, KY 42101	GPA: 3.44 SAT (ERW): 500-600 SAT (M): 480-580 ACT (C): 19-26 ED: No	Overall College Admit Rate: 98% Undergrad Enrollment: 15,286 Total Enrollment: 17,517	BA Photojournalism	Portfolio not req.
Louisiana Tech University 1310 West Railroad Avenue, Ruston, Louisiana 71272	GPA: 3.56 SAT (ERW): 530-640 SAT (M): 530-630 ACT (C): 22-28 ED: No	Overall College Admit Rate: 64% Undergrad Enrollment: 10,013 Total Enrollment: 11,126	BFA Studio Art, concentration: Photography	Portfolio not req.
University of Central Oklahoma 100 N University Dr, Edmond, OK 73034	GPA: N/A SAT (ERW): N/A SAT (M): N/A ACT (C): 18-24 ED: No	Overall College Admit Rate: 80% Undergrad Enrollment: 12,564 Total Enrollment: 14,132	BA Photographic Arts	Portfolio not req.
Maryland Institute College of Art (MICA) 1300 W. Mount Royal Ave., Baltimore, MD 21217	GPA: N/A SAT (ERW): N/A SAT (M): N/A ACT (C): N/A *Test-optional ED: Yes	Admit Rate: 90% Undergrad Enrollment: 1,331 Total Enrollment: 1,892	BFA Photography	Portfolio req.

SOUTH

PHOTOGRAPHY PROGRAMS

School	Avg. GPA, SAT Evidence-Based Reading Writing (ERW), SAT Math (M), and ACT Composite (C) Early Decision (ED): Yes/No	Admission Statistics	Program(s)	Portfolio Required (req.)
Sam Houston State University 1905 University Ave, Huntsville, TX 77340	GPA: N/A SAT (ERW): 490-570 SAT (M): 480-550 ACT (C): 18-23 ED: No	Overall College Admit Rate: 92% Undergrad Enrollment: 18,811 Total Enrollment: 21,912	BFA Photography	Portfolio req.
Texas Christian University (TCU) 2800 South University Dr., Fort Worth, TX 76109	GPA: N/A SAT (ERW): 560-660 SAT (M): 550-660 ACT (C): 25-31 ED: No	Overall College Admit Rate: 48% Undergrad Enrollment: 9,704 Total Enrollment: 11,379	BA Studio Art, concentration: Photography BFA Studio Art, concentration: Photography	Portfolio req.
Texas State University 601 University Dr, San Marcos, TX 78666	GPA: N/A SAT (ERW): 510-600 SAT (M): 500-580 ACT (C): 20-25 ED: No	Overall College Admit Rate: 85% Undergrad Enrollment: 33,193 Total Enrollment: 37,812	BFA Photography	Portfolio not req.
University of Houston 4200 Elgin Street, Room 122, Houston, TX 77204	GPA: 3.73 SAT (ERW): 560-650 SAT (M): 560-660 ACT (C): 22-28 ED: No	Overall College Admit Rate: 63% Undergrad Enrollment: 39,165 Total Enrollment: 47,090	BFA Studio Art, concentration: Photography & Digital Media	Portfolio req.
Virginia Commonwealth University Virginia Commonwealth University, Richmond, VA 23284	GPA: 3.72 SAT (ERW): 540-640 SAT (M): 520-610 ACT (C): 21-28 ED: No	Admit Rate: 91% Undergrad Enrollment: 21,943 Total Enrollment: 29,070	BFA Photography & Film, concentration: Photography	Portfolio req.

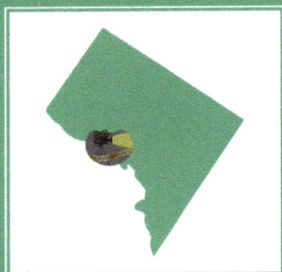

ALABAMA

ARKANSAS

DELAWARE

DISTRICT OF
COLUMBIA

FLORIDA

GEORGIA

KENTUCKY

LOUISIANA

MARYLAND

MISSISSIPPI

NORTH CAROLINA

OKLAHOMA

SOUTH CAROLINA

TENNESSEE

TEXAS

VIRGINIA

WEST VIRGINIA

THE GEORGE WASHINGTON UNIVERSITY

Address: 814 20th Street NW, 3rd Floor, Washington, DC 20052
Website: *https://corcoran.gwu.edu/photojournalism-undergraduate*
Contact: *https://corcoran.gwu.edu/contact*
Phone: (202) 994-1700
Email: corcoranschool@gwu.edu

COST OF ATTENDANCE:

Tuition & Fees: $59,780 | **Additional Expenses:** $19,540
Total: $79,320

Financial Aid: https://financialaid.gwu.edu/

ADDITIONAL INFORMATION:

Available Degree(s)

- BFA Photojournalism
- BA Fine Arts, concentration: Photojournalism

Portfolio Requirement

The BA in Fine Arts does not require a portfolio. However, it is required for the BFA. Furthermore, all students must submit a portfolio if they want to be considered for Corcoran Scholars. Submit 12-20 works via SlideRoom.

Scholarships Offered

Students who are admitted as Corcoran Scholars receive a renewable award. Furthermore, all GWU students may be eligible for Presidential Academic Scholarships, the Cisneros Scholars program, or the International Baccalaureate (IB) Scholarship. No additional application is necessary to be considered for the Presidential Academic Scholarship.

Special Opportunities

The photojournalism program offers a multidisciplinary approach to visual media and documentary work. Students in the program are taught studio art practices and the traditions of the field from the first year onwards. GWU is located in the heart of Washington, D.C., and as such, students in this program have a unique opportunity to engage in experiential learning experiences and internships.

Notable Alumni

Cynthia Connolly, John Edmonds, J.W. Faul, Avi Gupta, Robert Hite, Evan Hume, Kim Kirkpatrick, David Keith Lynch, Kesi Marcus, Romy Willing, and Firooz Zahedi

UNIVERSITY OF CENTRAL FLORIDA

Address: 4000 Central Florida Blvd, Orlando, FL 32816
Website: *https://svad.cah.ucf.edu/academics/photography/*
Contact: *https://www.ucf.edu/admissions/undergraduate/contact*
Phone: (844) 376-9160
Email: admission@ucf.edu

COST OF ATTENDANCE:

In-State Tuition & Fees: $5,944 | **Additional Expenses:** $16,180
Total: $22,124

Out-of-State Tuition & Fees: $20,969 | **Additional Expenses:** $16,180
Total: $37,149

Financial Aid: https://www.ucf.edu/services/s/financial-aid/

ADDITIONAL INFORMATION:

Available Degree(s)

- BA Art: Studio, Specialization: Photography
- BFA Studio Art, Specialization: Photography

Portfolio Requirement

There is no portfolio requirement for incoming students.

Scholarships Offered

All students are automatically considered for the Pegasus Scholarships. These merit-based scholarships are renewable and include the National Merit Scholarships, the Provost Scholarship, the Pegasus Gold, Silver, & Bronze Scholarships, and many more.

Special Opportunities

UCF also offers a BS in Photography for students who earn their AS in Photographic Technology from Daytona State College. BFA students must first apply to the BA Art: Studio first. Then, after successful completion of the portfolio review, they may apply to the BFA program.

Notable Alumni

Daniel Myrick and Nancy Yasecko

ALABAMA
ARKANSAS
DELAWARE
DISTRICT OF COLUMBIA
FLORIDA
GEORGIA
KENTUCKY
LOUISIANA
MARYLAND
MISSISSIPPI
NORTH CAROLINA
OKLAHOMA
SOUTH CAROLINA
TENNESSEE
TEXAS
VIRGINIA
WEST VIRGINIA

SOUTH

ALABAMA

ARKANSAS

DELAWARE

DISTRICT OF
COLUMBIA

FLORIDA

GEORGIA

KENTUCKY

LOUISIANA

MARYLAND

MISSISSIPPI

NORTH CAROLINA

OKLAHOMA

SOUTH CAROLINA

TENNESSEE

TEXAS

VIRGINIA

WEST VIRGINIA

UNIVERSITY OF MIAMI

Address: 1223 Dickinson Drive, Coral Gables, FL 33146
Website: *https://art.as.miami.edu/programs/undergraduate-programs/photography/index.html*
Contact: *https://admissions.miami.edu/undergraduate/about/contact-us/index.html*
Phone: (305) 284 3731
Email: admission@miami.edu

COST OF ATTENDANCE:

Tuition & Fees: $53,682 | **Additional Expenses:** $20,030
Total: $73,712

Financial Aid: https://finaid.miami.edu/index.html

ADDITIONAL INFORMATION:

Available Degree(s)

- BA Art, specialization: Photography
- BA Studio Art, specialization: Photography
- BFA Art, specialization: Photography

Portfolio Requirement

There is no portfolio requirement for incoming students.

Scholarships Offered

The most prestigious merit award at UMiami is the Stamps Scholarship. This scholarship covers the student's full cost of attendance for four years of study, including a laptop allowance and access to a $12,000 enrichment fund that may be used towards educational purposes. Other UM scholarships also cover the full cost of tuition or cost of attendance for all four years. These are all based on merit and/or financial need.

Special Opportunities

The photography program at UMiami is strongly focused on digital imaging. Students improve their studio techniques, learn how to utilize digital technology, and use the darkroom facilities.

Notable Alumni

Patrick Farrell and Arnold Newman

SAVANNAH COLLEGE OF ART & DESIGN (SCAD)

Address: 342 Bull St., Savannah, GA 31401
Website: *https://www.scad.edu/academics/programs/photography*
Contact: *https://www.scad.edu/about/contact*
Phone: (912) 525-5100
Email: contact@scad.edu
Other locations: Atlanta, GA

COST OF ATTENDANCE:

Tuition & Fees: $38,340 | **Additional Expenses:** $15,269
Total: $53,609

Financial Aid: https://www.scad.edu/admission/financial-aid-and-scholarships

ADDITIONAL INFORMATION:

Available Degree(s)

- BA Photography
- BFA Photography

Portfolio Requirement

Portfolios are required for incoming students. Portfolios do not need to reflect the student's intended major. Submit 10-20 visual art works, 3-5 minutes of time-based media, or submit a mixture of the two options.

Scholarships Offered

All applicants including international students are eligible for merit-scholarships. The May and Paul Poetter Scholarship awards full tuition and is based on academic achievement. The Frances Larkin McCommon Scholarship awards full tuition and is based on artistic achievement. SCAD also offers SCAD academic scholarships ($1,500-$12,000). Among grants, the SCAD Athletic Grant awards $2,000-$12,000. Furthermore, students may receive a scholarship award via the SCAD Challenge Scholarship. Awards range from $2,000-$4,000.

Special Opportunities

Both degrees are available on campus at the Atlanta and Savannah campuses as well as online. Photography students have access to premium tools and facilities, such as full black-and-white darkrooms, professional-level cameras, shooting studios, film processing labs, studio lighting kits, printers, Adobe Creative Cloud, and more.

Notable Alumni

Andrew Phillips and Claire Rosen

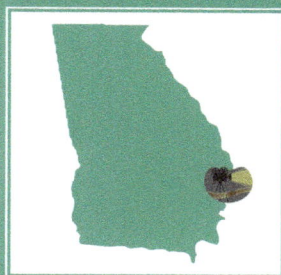

ALABAMA
ARKANSAS
DELAWARE
DISTRICT OF COLUMBIA
FLORIDA
GEORGIA
KENTUCKY
LOUISIANA
MARYLAND
MISSISSIPPI
NORTH CAROLINA
OKLAHOMA
SOUTH CAROLINA
TENNESSEE
TEXAS
VIRGINIA
WEST VIRGINIA

SOUTH

ALABAMA

ARKANSAS

DELAWARE

DISTRICT OF
COLUMBIA

FLORIDA

GEORGIA

KENTUCKY

LOUISIANA

MARYLAND

MISSISSIPPI

NORTH CAROLINA

OKLAHOMA

SOUTH CAROLINA

TENNESSEE

TEXAS

VIRGINIA

WEST VIRGINIA

WESTERN KENTUCKY UNIVERSITY

Address: 1906 College Heights Blvd, Bowling Green, KY 42101
Website: *https://www.wku.edu/schoolofmedia/
undergraduateprograms/photojournalism/photojournalism.php*
Contact: *https://www.wku.edu/admissions/contactus.php*
Phone: (270) 745-2551
Email: https://www.wku.edu/admissions/ask/index.php

COST OF ATTENDANCE:

In-State Tuition & Fees: $10,992 | **Additional Expenses:** $13,645
Total: $24,637

Out-of-State Tuition & Fees: $27,000 | **Additional Expenses:** $13,645
Total: $40,645

Financial Aid: https://www.wku.edu/financialaid/

ADDITIONAL INFORMATION:

Available Degree(s)

- BA Photojournalism

Portfolio Requirement

There is no portfolio requirement for incoming students.

Scholarships Offered

WKU offers numerous merit-based and need-based scholarships.
The Cherry Presidential Scholarship is available to applicants with
an unweighted GPA of 3.8 and a completed university application by
December 1st. No separate application is required. The award is up
to $16,000 per year, annually.

Special Opportunities

The photojournalism program at WKU is a documentary
photography major that introduces students to content-driven
image practices for paper and electronic publications. Graduates
from this program have won the William Randolph Hearst national
photojournalism championship 19 out of 21 years.

Notable Alumni

Leslye Davis, Naomi Driessnack, Harrison Hill, Inge Hooker, Kristen
Houser, Julie Jenkins, Rick Loomis, Alixandra Mattingly, Katie Meek,
Kendall Norwood, Samuel Oldenburg, Sawyer Smith, and Megan
Tan

LOUISIANA TECH UNIVERSITY

Address: 1310 West Railroad Avenue, Ruston, Louisiana 71272
Website: *http://design.latech.edu/photography/*
Contact: *https://www.latech.edu/admissions/*
Phone: (318) 257-3036
Email: communications@latech.edu

COST OF ATTENDANCE:

In-State Tuition & Fees: $9,645 | **Additional Expenses:** $10,719
Total: $20,364

Out-of-State Tuition & Fees: $18,558 | **Additional Expenses:** $10,719
Total: $29,277

Financial Aid: https://www.latech.edu/current-students/financial-aid/

ADDITIONAL INFORMATION:

Available Degree(s)

- BFA Studio Art, concentration: Photography

Portfolio Requirement

There is no portfolio requirement for incoming students.

Scholarships Offered

Louisiana Tech offers merit-based and need-based scholarships. No separate application is necessary, so long as the applicant submits their university application by the priority deadline. Students may receive up to $9,500 per year, based on their test scores and GPA.

Special Opportunities

Studio art students receive extensive training in various studio mediums, whether 2D or 3D. In the first year, all students are taught the fundamentals of drawing, color theory, and 3D design. Later in the program, students declare a concentration. Photography facilities at Louisiana Tech include a lighting studio, digital photography classroom, an analog lab, printers, scanners, a large darkroom, and two private darkrooms.

ALABAMA

ARKANSAS

DELAWARE

DISTRICT OF COLUMBIA

FLORIDA

GEORGIA

KENTUCKY

LOUISIANA

MARYLAND

MISSISSIPPI

NORTH CAROLINA

OKLAHOMA

SOUTH CAROLINA

TENNESSEE

TEXAS

VIRGINIA

WEST VIRGINIA

SOUTH

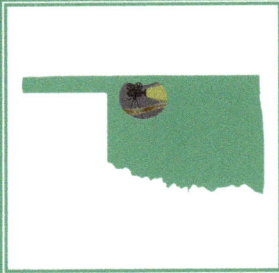

ALABAMA

ARKANSAS

DELAWARE

DISTRICT OF
COLUMBIA

FLORIDA

GEORGIA

KENTUCKY

LOUISIANA

MARYLAND

MISSISSIPPI

NORTH CAROLINA

OKLAHOMA

SOUTH CAROLINA

TENNESSEE

TEXAS

VIRGINIA

WEST VIRGINIA

UNIVERSITY OF CENTRAL OKLAHOMA

Address: 100 N University Dr, Edmond, OK 73034
Website: *https://www.uco.edu/programs/cla/program-photographic-arts-major*
Contact: *https://www.uco.edu/contact-us*
Phone: (405) 974-2727
Email: https://www.uco.edu/contact-us

COST OF ATTENDANCE:

In-State Tuition & Fees: $5,432 | **Additional Expenses:** $15,242
Total: $20,674

Out-of-State Tuition & Fees: $13,384 | **Additional Expenses:** $15,242
Total: $28,626

Financial Aid: https://www.uco.edu/admissions-aid/financial-aid/

ADDITIONAL INFORMATION:

Available Degree(s)

- BA Photographic Arts

Portfolio Requirement

There is no portfolio requirement for incoming students.

Scholarships Offered

All students are considered for academic, leadership, Oklahoma State Regents, and Higher Education scholarships upon submission of their application. No separate scholarship application is required. Some scholarships require an interview and students are notified of the requirement if they are in the running for an award.

Special Opportunities

The photography program at UCO has students learn about the aesthetics of a contemporary approach to their work. Students present their portfolio of work in a public forum, engage in self-exploration, and learn about the image-making process.

Notable Alumni

Jim Trosper

MARYLAND INSTITUTE COLLEGE OF ART (MICA)

Address: 1300 W. Mount Royal Ave., Baltimore, MD 21217
Website: *https://www.mica.edu/undergraduate-majors-minors/photography-major/*
Contact: *https://www.mica.edu/mica-dna/contact-us/*
Phone: (410) 669-9200
Email: https://www.mica.edu/forms/contact-undergraduate-admission/

COST OF ATTENDANCE:

Tuition & Fees: $53,333 | **Additional Expenses:** $17,820
Total: $71,153

Financial Aid: https://www.mica.edu/financial-aid/

ADDITIONAL INFORMATION:

Available Degree(s)

* BFA Photography

Portfolio Requirement

Portfolios are required for incoming students. Submit 12-20 works via the Common App.

Scholarships Offered

MICA offers several, competitive merit-based scholarships to all incoming undergraduate students. Some of these offers include the Mathias J. Devito Scholarship Program ($40,000 over 4 years), the Fanny B. Thalheimer Scholarship ($16,000-$68,000 over four years), the Academic Excellence Scholarships ($12,000-$24,000) and several others.

Special Opportunities

The photography program at MICA was established over 100 years ago. Students in this program learn about the history of photography, alternative darkroom processes, traditional techniques, and new techniques as well. One course in the program is titled "Picturing the Third Dimension", where students investigate what constitutes a photograph.

Notable Alumni

Joan Cassis, Linda Day Clark, Lola Flash, Marilyn Nance, and Dana Veraldi

ALABAMA
ARKANSAS
DELAWARE
DISTRICT OF COLUMBIA
FLORIDA
GEORGIA
KENTUCKY
LOUISIANA
MARYLAND
MISSISSIPPI
NORTH CAROLINA
OKLAHOMA
SOUTH CAROLINA
TENNESSEE
TEXAS
VIRGINIA
WEST VIRGINIA

SOUTH

ALABAMA

ARKANSAS

DELAWARE

DISTRICT OF COLUMBIA

FLORIDA

GEORGIA

KENTUCKY

LOUISIANA

MARYLAND

MISSISSIPPI

NORTH CAROLINA

OKLAHOMA

SOUTH CAROLINA

TENNESSEE

TEXAS

VIRGINIA

WEST VIRGINIA

SAM HOUSTON STATE UNIVERSITY

Address: 1905 University Ave, Huntsville, TX 77340
Website: *https://www.shsu.edu/programs/bachelor-of-fine-arts-in-photography/*
Contact: *https://www.shsu.edu/admissions/*
Phone: (936) 294-1828
Email: admissions@shsu.edu

COST OF ATTENDANCE:

In-State Tuition & Fees: $11,034 | **Additional Expenses:** $15,652
Total: $26,686

Out-of-State Tuition & Fees: $23,274 | **Additional Expenses:** $15,652
Total: $38,926

Financial Aid: https://www.shsu.edu/dept/financial-aid/

ADDITIONAL INFORMATION:

Available Degree(s)

- BFA Photography

Portfolio Requirement

Portfolios are required for incoming students. Submit 8-10 works that reflect conceptual and technical development.

Scholarships Offered

Applicants must apply separately for scholarships through the Scholarships4Kats Portal. Scholarships are based on merit and need, and range in value.

Special Opportunities

Students must successfully complete the Workshop in Art Studio and History (WASH) and pass a portfolio review at the end of their second year in order to proceed with the BFA program. Photography students learn technical and visual skills and find their own path in the field.

Notable Alumni

Frank Q. Dobbs and Richard Linklater

TEXAS CHRISTIAN UNIVERSITY (TCU)

Address: 2800 South University Dr., Fort Worth, TX 76109
Website: *https://finearts.tcu.edu/art/academics/areas-of-study/studio-art/*
Contact: *https://admissions.tcu.edu/connect.php*
Phone: (817) 257-7000
Email: frogmail@tcu.edu

COST OF ATTENDANCE:

Tuition & Fees: $51,660 | **Additional Expenses:** $20,168
Total: $71,828

Financial Aid: https://financialaid.tcu.edu/

ADDITIONAL INFORMATION:

Available Degree(s)

- BA Studio Art, concentration: Photography
- BFA Studio Art, concentration: Photography

Portfolio Requirement

Portfolios are required for incoming students. Submit 15-20 works that include drawings from observation.

Scholarships Offered

The Nordan Fine Arts Awards are competitive scholarships for students in the College of Fine Arts. The Nordan Young Artist Award is $10,000+ for incoming freshmen, based on application audition. Students may then renew this scholarship for their remaining years.

Special Opportunities

Students may volunteer or intern as gallery attendants at either of TCU's two galleries - the Moudy Gallery or the Fort Worth Contemporary Arts.

Notable Alumni

Linda Kaye, James Kerwin, and Bob Schieffer

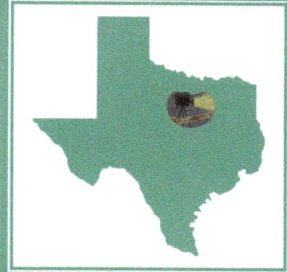

ALABAMA
ARKANSAS
DELAWARE
DISTRICT OF COLUMBIA
FLORIDA
GEORGIA
KENTUCKY
LOUISIANA
MARYLAND
MISSISSIPPI
NORTH CAROLINA
OKLAHOMA
SOUTH CAROLINA
TENNESSEE
TEXAS
VIRGINIA
WEST VIRGINIA

SOUTH

ALABAMA

ARKANSAS

DELAWARE

DISTRICT OF
COLUMBIA

FLORIDA

GEORGIA

KENTUCKY

LOUISIANA

MARYLAND

MISSISSIPPI

NORTH CAROLINA

OKLAHOMA

SOUTH CAROLINA

TENNESSEE

TEXAS

VIRGINIA

WEST VIRGINIA

TEXAS STATE UNIVERSITY

Address: 601 University Dr, San Marcos, TX 78666
Website: *https://www.finearts.txstate.edu/Art/academics/ undergrad/ugrad-dpi.html*
Contact: *https://www.theatreanddance.txstate.edu/About-the-Department/Contact-Us.html*
Phone: (512) 245-2111
Email: https://www.admissions.txstate.edu/contact.html

COST OF ATTENDANCE:

In-State Tuition & Fees: $11,540 | **Additional Expenses:** $15,080
Total: $26,620

Out-of-State Tuition & Fees: $23,820 | **Additional Expenses:** $15,080
Total: $38,900

Financial Aid: https://www.finaid.txstate.edu/

ADDITIONAL INFORMATION:

Available Degree(s)

- BFA Photography

Portfolio Requirement

There is no portfolio requirement for incoming students.

Scholarships Offered

Out-of-state students may qualify for a nonresident tuition waiver if they, "qualify for at least $1,000 in Texas State competitive or merit scholarships…". In addition, all applicants are automatically awarded National Scholarships and Assured scholarships when they gain acceptance to TSU. A number of competitive scholarships are available as well.

Special Opportunities

Photography students take coursework in traditional darkroom, advanced digital, readings in photography, contemporary photographic practices, and more. A senior capstone is required. Students also curate their portfolio over four years in preparation for professional life post-graduation.

Notable Alumni

Michael Curtis Asbill

UNIVERSITY OF HOUSTON

Address: 4200 Elgin Street, Room 122, Houston, TX 77204
Website: *https://www.uh.edu/kgmca/art/undergraduate-programs/photography-digital-media/*
Contact: *https://www.uh.edu/undergraduate-admissions/discover/meet-your-counselor/*
Phone: (713) 743-2400
Email: admissions@uh.edu

COST OF ATTENDANCE:

In-State Tuition & Fees: $11,569 | **Additional Expenses:** $11,110
Total: $22,679

Out-of-State Tuition & Fees: $26,839 | **Additional Expenses:** $11,110 **Total:** $37,949

Financial Aid: https://uh.edu/undergraduate-admissions/cost/index.php

ADDITIONAL INFORMATION:

Available Degree(s)

- BFA Studio Art, concentration: Photography & Digital Media

Portfolio Requirement

Portfolios are required for incoming students. Submit 2-4 examples of work created within the past two years. Applicants must also submit a 250-word statement of intent.

Scholarships Offered

University scholarships based on merit and/or demonstrated need are available to all students. For instance, the Academic Excellence scholarship gifts an award of up to $6,000 per year.

Special Opportunities

The Photography and Digital Media program teaches students technical, historical, and critical skills in relation to studio practice. Photography students with a strong GPA are encouraged to submit proposals to the area coordinator to earn internships with the various alternative spaces, non-profits, and museums in the Houston area.

Notable Alumni

Carll Goodpasture and Julian Schnabel

ALABAMA
ARKANSAS
DELAWARE
DISTRICT OF COLUMBIA
FLORIDA
GEORGIA
KENTUCKY
LOUISIANA
MARYLAND
MISSISSIPPI
NORTH CAROLINA
OKLAHOMA
SOUTH CAROLINA
TENNESSEE
TEXAS
VIRGINIA
WEST VIRGINIA

SOUTH

VIRGINIA COMMONWEALTH UNIVERSITY

Address: Virginia Commonwealth University, Richmond, VA 23284
Website: *https://arts.vcu.edu/academics/departments/photography-film/photography-bfa/*
Contact: *https://www.vcu.edu/contacts/*
Phone: (804) 828-0100
Email: ugrad@vcu.edu

COST OF ATTENDANCE:

In-State Tuition & Fees: $17,140 | **Additional Expenses:** $17,549
Total: $34,689

Out-of-State Tuition & Fees: $38,478 | **Additional Expenses:** $17,549
Total: $56,027

Financial Aid: https://finaid.vcu.edu/

ADDITIONAL INFORMATION:

Available Degree(s)

- BFA Photography & Film, concentration: Photography

Portfolio Requirement

Portfolios are required for incoming students. Submit 12-16 works created within the past two years. Drawing from observation is encouraged, and copying character designs or another artist's work is strongly discouraged.

Scholarships Offered

First-year students may be eligible for VCUarts talent scholarships ($5,000-$12,000 annually) if they apply by January 15th. Students are automatically considered and eligibility is based on academic merit and artistic talent. In addition, all students are automatically considered for institutional scholarships if they apply by November 15th. University scholarship awards vary based on the scholarship, but range from $8,000 per year to $16,000 plus room and board per year.

Special Opportunities

Photography students graduate with a capstone photography portfolio, curated over the previous four years. Classes include darkroom, digital imaging, writing for the screen, sound & color, and professional practice. Furthermore, students have access to premium facilities such as the 24/7 digital labs along with state-of-the-art equipment.

Notable Alumni

Macon Blair and Tony Cokes

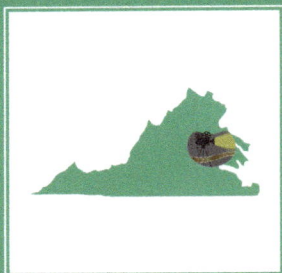

ALABAMA
ARKANSAS
DELAWARE
DISTRICT OF COLUMBIA
FLORIDA
GEORGIA
KENTUCKY
LOUISIANA
MARYLAND
MISSISSIPPI
NORTH CAROLINA
OKLAHOMA
SOUTH CAROLINA
TENNESSEE
TEXAS
VIRGINIA
WEST VIRGINIA

ALASKA

ARIZONA

CALIFORNIA

COLORADO

HAWAII

IDAHO

MONTANA

NEVADA

NEW MEXICO

OREGON

UTAH

WASHINGTON

WYOMING

CHAPTER 14

REGION FOUR

WEST

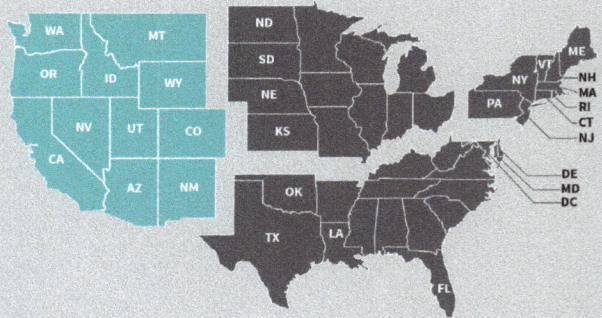

12 *Programs* | 13 *States*

1. *AZ – Arizona State University*
2. *CA - Academy of Art University*
3. *CA - ArtCenter College of Design*
4. *CA - California College of the Arts (CCA)*
5. *CA - California Institute of the Arts*
6. *CA - California State University, Long Beach*
7. *CA - California State University, Sacramento*
8. *CA - Fashion Institute of Design and Merchandising*
9. *CA - Pacific Union College*
10. *OR - University of Oregon*
11. *UT - Brigham Young University*
12. *WA - University of Washington*

PHOTOGRAPHY PROGRAMS

School	Avg. GPA, SAT Evidence-Based Reading Writing (ERW), SAT Math (M), and ACT Composite (C) Early Decision (ED): Yes/No	Admission Statistics	Program(s)	Portfolio Required (req.)
Arizona State University 1151 S. Forest Ave. Tempe, AZ 85281	GPA: N/A SAT (ERW): 550-650 SAT (M): 550-670 ACT (C): 21-28 *Test-optional ED: No	Admit Rate: 88% Undergrad Enrollment: 63,124 Total Enrollment: 74,795	BFA Photography	Portfolio not req.
Academy of Art University 79 New Montgomery St., San Francisco, CA 94105	GPA: N/A SAT (ERW): N/A SAT (M): N/A ACT (C): N/A *Academy of Art has an open admissions policy. ED: No	Admit Rate: N/A Undergrad Enrollment: 6,124 Total Enrollment: 8,928 Program Completion (2020): 29	BFA Photography	Portfolio not req.
ArtCenter College of Design 1700 Lida St, Pasadena, CA 91103	GPA: N/A SAT (ERW): N/A* SAT (M): N/A* ACT (C): N/A* *Test-optional ED: No	Overall College Admit Rate: 76% Undergrad Enrollment: 1,912 Total Enrollment: 2,182	BFA Photography and Imaging	Portfolio req.

School	Avg. GPA, SAT Evidence-Based Reading Writing (ERW), SAT Math (M), and ACT Composite (C) Early Decision (ED): Yes/No	Admission Statistics	Program(s)	Portfolio Required (req.)
California College of the Arts (CCA) 1111 Eighth St., San Francisco, CA 94107	GPA: N/A SAT (ERW): N/A* SAT (M): N/A* ACT (C): N/A* *Test-optional ED: No	Overall College Admit Rate: 85% Undergrad Enrollment: 1,239 Total Enrollment: 1,612	BFA Photography and Imaging	Portfolio req.
California Institute of the Arts (CalArts) 24700 McBean Pkwy., Valencia, CA 91355	GPA: N/A SAT (ERW): N/A* SAT (M): N/A* ACT (C): N/A* *Test-optional ED: Yes	Overall College Admit Rate: 32% Undergrad Enrollment: 783 Total Enrollment: 1,189	BFA Photography and Media	Portfolio req.
California State University, Long Beach (CSULB) 1250 Bellflower Boulevard, Long Beach, CA 90840	GPA: 3.68 SAT (ERW): 510-620 SAT (M): 510-620 ACT (C): 20-26 ED: No	Admit Rate: 42% Undergrad Enrollment: 34,216 Total Enrollment: 40,069	BFA Art, Option: Photography	Portfolio not req. for first-years
California State University, Sacramento 6000 J St, Sacramento, CA 95819	GPA: 3.41 SAT (ERW): 470-570 SAT (M): 460-560 ACT (C): 17-23 ED: No	Admit Rate: 83% Undergrad Enrollment: 29,296 Total Enrollment: 32,293	BFA Photography	Portfolio not req.

WEST

PHOTOGRAPHY PROGRAMS

School	Avg. GPA, SAT Evidence-Based Reading Writing (ERW), SAT Math (M), and ACT Composite (C) Early Decision (ED): Yes/No	Admission Statistics	Program(s)	Portfolio Required (req.)
Fashion Institute of Design and Merchandising (FIDM) 919 S. Grand Ave., Los Angeles, CA 90015	GPA: N/A SAT (ERW): N/A SAT (M): N/A ACT (C): N/A ED: No	Admit Rate: 39% Undergrad Enrollment: 1,847 Total Enrollment: 1,886	BA Digital Media	Portfolio req.
Pacific Union College One Angwin Ave, Angwin, CA 94508	GPA: N/A SAT (ERW): 460-580 SAT (M): 440-560 ACT (C): 17-24 ED: No	Admit Rate: 59% Undergrad Enrollment: 955 Total Enrollment: 959	BA Art, emphasis: Photography	Portfolio not req.
University of Oregon 5249 University of Oregon, Eugene, OR 97403	GPA: 3.65 SAT (ERW): 550-650 SAT (M): 540-640 ACT (C): 22-29 ED: No	Overall College Admit Rate: 84% Undergrad Enrollment: 18,045 Total Enrollment: 21,752	BFA Art, concentration: Photography	Portfolio req.
Brigham Young University Brigham Young University, Provo, UT 84602	GPA: 3.86 SAT (ERW): 610-700 SAT (M): 590-710 ACT (C): 26-32 ED: No	Admit Rate: 69% Undergrad Enrollment: 33,365 Total Enrollment: 36,450	BFA Photo- & Lens-Based Design	Portfolio not req.

School	Avg. GPA, SAT Evidence-Based Reading Writing (ERW), SAT Math (M), and ACT Composite (C) Early Decision (ED): Yes/No	Admission Statistics	Program(s)	Portfolio Required (req.)
University of Washington 1400 NE Campus Parkway, Seattle, WA, 98195	GPA: 3.82 SAT (ERW): 590-700 SAT (M): 610-753 ACT (C): 27-33 ED: No	Overall College Admit Rate: 56% Undergrad Enrollment: 32,244 Total Enrollment: 48,149	BA Art, concentration: Photo/Media	Portfolio not req.

WEST

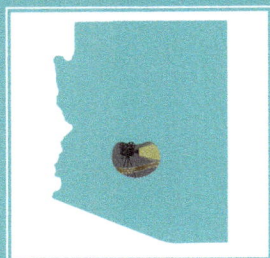

ALASKA

ARIZONA

CALIFORNIA

COLORADO

HAWAII

IDAHO

MONTANA

NEVADA

NEW MEXICO

OREGON

UTAH

WASHINGTON

WYOMING

ARIZONA STATE UNIVERSITY

Address: 1151 S. Forest Ave. Tempe, AZ 85281
Website: *https://art.asu.edu/degree-programs/ photography?dept=160349&id=1*
Contact: *https://admission.asu.edu/findmyrep*
Phone: (480) 965-7788
Email: admissions@asu.edu

COST OF ATTENDANCE:

In-State Tuition & Fees: $10,710 | **Additional Expenses:** $20,811
Total: $31,521

Out-of-State Tuition & Fees: $28,800 | **Additional Expenses:** $21,561
Total: $50,361

Financial Aid: https://students.asu.edu/financial-aid

ADDITIONAL INFORMATION:

Available Degree(s)

- BFA Photography

Portfolio Requirement

There is no portfolio requirement for incoming students.

Scholarships Offered

ASU offers many merit-based and need-based scholarships for all students. The New American University Scholars is for high achieving students. This award is for residents, nonresidents, transfer students, and international students.

Special Opportunities

In the photography program, students explore technical skills as well as a historical analysis of the medium. Interdisciplinary opportunities are available in printmaking, intermedia, sculpture, and more. ASU also offers an online version of their photography program.

Notable Alumni

Stefan Springman and Ross Thomas

ACADEMY OF ART UNIVERSITY

Address: 79 New Montgomery St., San Francisco, CA 94105
Website: *https://www.academyart.edu/degree/photography/?degree=bfa*
Contact: *https://my.academyart.edu/directories/admissions*
Phone: (800) 544-2787
Email: admissions@academyart.edu

COST OF ATTENDANCE:

Tuition & Fees: $26,399 | **Additional Expenses:** N/A
Total: $26,399

Financial Aid: https://www.academyart.edu/finances/types-of-financial-aid/

ADDITIONAL INFORMATION:

Available Degree(s)

- BFA Photography

Portfolio Requirement

There is no portfolio requirement for incoming students.

Scholarships Offered

The Emerging Artist Scholarship offers awards up to $3,000.
International Art & Design Scholarship awards a limited number of
scholarships (up to $2,000) to international students.

Special Opportunities

Photography students work towards building their professional
portfolio - which will be the main component to help them gain
employment post-graduation. Students may choose a focus on
commercial or editorial, fine art, or documentary photography.

Notable Alumni

Scott Borrero, Deanne Fitzmaurice, and Chris Milk

ALASKA

ARIZONA

CALIFORNIA

COLORADO

HAWAII

IDAHO

MONTANA

NEVADA

NEW MEXICO

OREGON

UTAH

WASHINGTON

WYOMING

WEST

ALASKA

ARIZONA

CALIFORNIA

COLORADO

HAWAII

IDAHO

MONTANA

NEVADA

NEW MEXICO

OREGON

UTAH

WASHINGTON

WYOMING

ARTCENTER COLLEGE OF DESIGN

Address: 1700 Lida St, Pasadena, CA 91103
Website: *https://www.artcenter.edu/academics/undergraduate-degrees/photography-and-imaging/overview.html*
Contact: *http://www.artcenter.edu/admissions/contact.html*
Phone: (626) 396-2373
Email: admissions@artcenter.edu

COST OF ATTENDANCE:

Tuition & Fees: $49,653 | **Additional Expenses:** $24,820
Total: $74,473

Financial Aid: https://www.artcenter.edu/admissions/tuition-and-aid/tuition-and-fees/tuition.html

ADDITIONAL INFORMATION:

Available Degree(s)

- BFA Photography and Imaging

Portfolio Requirement

Portfolios are required for incoming students. Submit 20-25 black-and-white, color, or digital images that are intentional and have a specific point of view. Include a variety of subjects in various settings.

Scholarships Offered

ArtCenter awards merit-based and need-based scholarships to students. Students with an exceptional portfolio are awarded up to $25,000.

Special Opportunities

The photography program at ArtCenter is close-knit and focused. Students learn traditional and digital techniques. Students are encouraged to understand the sociocultural impacts on the medium and the historical progression of photography.

Notable Alumni

Andrew Bernstein, Lee Friedlander, Gizelle Hernandez, George Holtz, Melodie McDaniel, Sam Nava, Yuya Parker, Daria Kobayashi Ritch, Matthew Rolston, Jen Rosenstein, Andrea Sofia Santizo, Kit Sinclair, Hiroshi Sugimoto, Wesley Sun, Cedric Terrell, Yu Tsai, Kjell von Sice, and Glen Wexler

CALIFORNIA COLLEGE OF THE ARTS (CCA)

Address: 1111 Eighth St., San Francisco, CA 94107
Website: *https://www.cca.edu/fine-arts/photography/*
Contact: *Contact via phone or email.*
Phone: (800) 447-1278
Email: info@cca.edu

COST OF ATTENDANCE:

Tuition & Fees: $54,726 | **Additional Expenses:** $25,255
Total: $79,981

Financial Aid: https://www.cca.edu/admissions/tuition/#section-financial-aid

ADDITIONAL INFORMATION:

Available Degree(s)

- BFA Photography and Imaging

Portfolio Requirement

Portfolios are required for incoming students. Submit 10-15 works via SlideRoom.

Scholarships Offered

Merit-based, need-based, CCA-named, and other scholarships available.

Special Opportunities

Photography and Imaging students at CCA learn about various photographic methods, contemporary practices, and digital tools. CCA also offers a year-round artist lecture series where students learn from guest lecturers in photography and interdisciplinary arts.

Notable Alumni

Beatrice Helg, Todd Hido, Jim Ricks, Hank Willis Thomas, and Hulleah Tsinhnahjinnie

ALASKA

ARIZONA

CALIFORNIA

COLORADO

HAWAII

IDAHO

MONTANA

NEVADA

NEW MEXICO

OREGON

UTAH

WASHINGTON

WYOMING

WEST

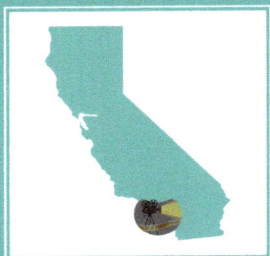

ALASKA

ARIZONA

CALIFORNIA

COLORADO

HAWAII

IDAHO

MONTANA

NEVADA

NEW MEXICO

OREGON

UTAH

WASHINGTON

WYOMING

CALIFORNIA INSTITUTE OF THE ARTS (CALARTS)

Address: 24700 McBean Pkwy., Valencia, CA 91355
Website: *https://art.calarts.edu/programs/photography-and-media/bfa*
Contact: *https://calarts.edu/about/contact*
Phone: (661) 255-1050
Email: admissions@calarts.edu

COST OF ATTENDANCE:

Tuition & Fees: $53,466 | **Additional Expenses:** $20,792
Total: $74,258

Financial Aid: https://calarts.edu/tuition-and-financial-aid/financial-aid/overview

ADDITIONAL INFORMATION:

Available Degree(s)

- BFA Photography and Media

Portfolio Requirement

Portfolios are required for incoming students. Submit 20 works in any medium. A variety of works is encouraged. An artist statement between 500-1000 words is also required.

Scholarships Offered

CalArts offers institutional scholarships that are awarded to students based on need and merit. All awards cover tuition only. In addition, they offer endowed and annually funded scholarships.

Special Opportunities

Photography and Media students are encouraged to challenge the conventional notions of what constitutes an image and to experiment with materials. Students engage in critical thinking and learning about theoretical concepts while also building their technical skills.

Notable Alumni

Sadie Barnette, Julie Becker, Cindy Bernard, Phil Chang, Anne Collier, Miles Coolidge, Zoe Crosher, Travis Diehl, Zackary Drucker, Todd Gray, Carla Herrera-Prats, Lyle Ashton Harris, Doug Ischar, Liz Larner, Miranda Lichtenstein, Karolina Karlic, Michael Mandiberg, Daniel J. Martinez, Josephine Meckseper, Nicole Miller, Carter Mull, Kelly Nipper, Catherine Opie, Alex Slade, Jan Tumlir, Carrie Mae Weems, and James Welling

CALIFORNIA STATE UNIVERSITY, LONG BEACH

Address: 1250 Bellflower Boulevard, Long Beach, CA 90840
Website: *https://www.csulb.edu/school-of-art/areas-of-study/studio-art/photography*
Contact: *https://www.csulb.edu/contact*
Phone: (562) 985-4111
Email: https://www.csulb.edu/contact

COST OF ATTENDANCE:

In-State Tuition & Fees: $6,846 | **Additional Expenses:** $18,206
Total: $25,386

Out-of-State Tuition & Fees: $17,142| **Additional Expenses:** $18,540
Total: $35,682

Financial Aid: https://www.csulb.edu/student-affairs/financial-aid-and-scholarships-office

ADDITIONAL INFORMATION:

Available Degree(s)

- BFA Art, Option: Photography

Portfolio Requirement

Portfolios are not required for incoming students when they apply from high school. However, they are required during the junior year.

Scholarships Offered

The President's Scholars Program offers merit-based scholarships to students admitted to the University Honors Program (UHP). Students may apply for BeachScholarships once they are admitted into CSULB.

Special Opportunities

Fine art photography is emphasized in CSULB's program. Digital and alternative techniques are taught. Facilities include a large black-and-white program, color printing area, and digital print facilities.

Notable Alumni

Coy Allen, Verne Carlson, Mark Steven Johnson, Joe Johnston, Tim Minear, Penelope Spheeris, and Stephen Spielberg

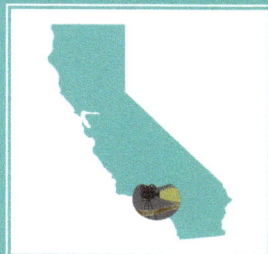

ALASKA

ARIZONA

CALIFORNIA

COLORADO

HAWAII

IDAHO

MONTANA

NEVADA

NEW MEXICO

OREGON

UTAH

WASHINGTON

WYOMING

WEST

ALASKA

ARIZONA

CALIFORNIA

COLORADO

HAWAII

IDAHO

MONTANA

NEVADA

NEW MEXICO

OREGON

UTAH

WASHINGTON

WYOMING

CALIFORNIA STATE UNIVERSITY, SACRAMENTO

Address: 6000 J St, Sacramento, CA 95819
Website: *https://www.csus.edu/college/arts-letters/design/design-programs.html#photography-program*
Contact: *https://www.csus.edu/apply/admissions/connect-with-admissions.html*
Phone: (916) 278-1000
Email: admissions@csus.edu

COST OF ATTENDANCE:

In-State Tuition & Fees: $7,368 | **Additional Expenses:** $19,764
Total: $27,132

Out-of-State Tuition & Fees: $16,872 | **Additional Expenses:** $19,764
Total: $36,636

Financial Aid: https://www.calstate.edu/attend/campuses/sacramento/Pages/cost-and-financial-aid.aspx

ADDITIONAL INFORMATION:

Available degree(s)

- BFA Photography

Portfolio Requirement

There is no portfolio requirement for incoming students.

Scholarships Offered

Sacramento State offers merit-based and need-based aid to students. A separate application may also be submitted to be matched with scholarships via the Sacramento State Scholarship Portal.

Special Opportunities

In the BFA Photography program at Sacramento State, students are educated in contemporary photographic methods and learn about the communicative effects of the medium. This program is for students interested in pursuing a career as photographic image makers. Students receive a liberal arts background along with professional preparation.

Notable Alumni

Joe Carnahan, Ryan Coogler Tom Hanks, Richard Montoya, Edward James Olmos, and Elaine Welteroth

FASHION INSTITUTE OF DESIGN AND MERCHANDISING (FIDM)

Address: 919 S. Grand Ave., Los Angeles, CA 90015
Website: *https://fidm.edu/en/majors/digital+media/*
Contact: https://fidm.edu/en/about/contact+us/
Phone: (800) 624-1200
Email: admissions@fidm.edu
Other locations: San Francisco, CA; Irvine, CA; San Diego, CA

COST OF ATTENDANCE:

Tuition & Fees: $31,465 | **Additional Expenses:** $22,373
Total: $53,838

Financial Aid: https://fidm.edu/en/admissions/financial+aid/

ADDITIONAL INFORMATION:

Available Degree(s)

- BA Digital Media

Portfolio Requirement

Portfolios are required for incoming students. Submit a portfolio project in response to a prompt with an essay or submit a two-minute video, 6 images, an Instagram page, or a podcast episode. FIDM is flexible with the portfolio submission, so applicants are advised to check their website regularly for updates and more information.

Scholarships Offered

The FCCLA National Scholarship Competition offers a full year of tuition to first place winners. In addition, high school juniors who are active members of the official FIDM Fashion Club are eligible to enter the FIDM Fashion Club Junior Scholarship Competition. High school seniors may be eligible for the FIDM National Scholarship Competition (covering one year of tuition).

Special Opportunities

Students first apply to the AA in Digital Media. Near the end of their AA program, they may apply to the BA in Digital Media. The Digital Media program trains students in digital cinema techniques as well as a foundation in filmmaking from pre-production through post-production.

Notable Alumni

Lisa Kristine

ALASKA

ARIZONA

CALIFORNIA

COLORADO

HAWAII

IDAHO

MONTANA

NEVADA

NEW MEXICO

OREGON

UTAH

WASHINGTON

WYOMING

WEST

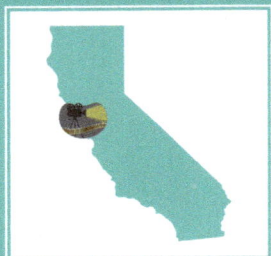

ALASKA

ARIZONA

CALIFORNIA

COLORADO

HAWAII

IDAHO

MONTANA

NEVADA

NEW MEXICO

OREGON

UTAH

WASHINGTON

WYOMING

PACIFIC UNION COLLEGE

Address: One Angwin Ave, Angwin, CA 94508
Website: *https://www.puc.edu/academics/departments/visual-arts*
Contact: *https://www.puc.edu/admissions-aid/admissions-process*
Phone: (800) 862-7080
Email: admissions@puc.edu

COST OF ATTENDANCE:

Tuition & Fees: $32,016 | **Additional Expenses:** $12,531
Total: $44,547

Financial Aid: https://www.puc.edu/admissions-aid/tuition-aid

ADDITIONAL INFORMATION:

Available degree(s)

- BA Art, emphasis: Photography

Portfolio Requirement

There is no portfolio requirement for incoming students.

Scholarships Offered

PUC offers many merit-based and need-based scholarships to students. The Maxwell Scholarship rewards incoming freshmen full tuition based on GPA and ACT/SAT scores. Other merit scholarships include the President's, Dean's, Trustee's, and Founder's scholarships.

Special Opportunities

The photography program at Pacific Union College educates students in technical skills as well as general artistic skills. Students build their portfolio over four years which will ultimately help them start their career upon graduation.

Notable Alumni

Jerry Dodrill, Jeffrey C. Gleason, Jennifer-Finnley Kirkman, and Brian Kyle

UNIVERSITY OF OREGON

Address: 5249 University of Oregon, Eugene, OR 97403
Website: *https://artdesign.uoregon.edu/art/undergrad/media-areas#photography*
Contact: *https://admissions.uoregon.edu/contact*
Phone: (541) 346-3656
Email: admissions@uoregon.edu

COST OF ATTENDANCE:

In-State Tuition & Fees: $15,054 | **Additional Expenses:** $14,640
Total: $29,694

Out-of-State Tuition & Fees: $41,700 | **Additional Expenses:** $14,640
Total: $56,340

Financial Aid: https://financialaid.uoregon.edu/

ADDITIONAL INFORMATION:

Available Degree(s)

- BFA Art, concentration: Photography

Portfolio Requirement

Portfolios are required for incoming students.

Scholarships Offered

The Architects Foundation Diversity Scholarships, need-based aid, and university-wide scholarships offer varying award amounts and opportunities. University-wide scholarships include the Stamps Scholarship (four years of full tuition, fees, room & board, and up to $12,000 in enrichment funds), the Presidential Scholarship ($36,000 over four years), Diversity Excellence Scholarship ($6500), and more.

Special Opportunities

Coursework emphasizes concept and context. Students learn a diverse range of coursework within the medium, such as The Photographic Book, Alternative Processes, Conceptual Strategies, Film & Darkroom, and more.

Notable Alumni

Jake Swantko and Russel Wong

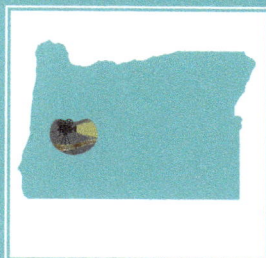

ALASKA

ARIZONA

CALIFORNIA

COLORADO

HAWAII

IDAHO

MONTANA

NEVADA

NEW MEXICO

OREGON

UTAH

WASHINGTON

WYOMING

WEST

ALASKA

ARIZONA

CALIFORNIA

COLORADO

HAWAII

IDAHO

MONTANA

NEVADA

NEW MEXICO

OREGON

UTAH

WASHINGTON

WYOMING

BRIGHAM YOUNG UNIVERSITY

Address: Brigham Young University, Provo, UT 84602
Website: *https://designdept.byu.edu/photography*
Contact: *https://enrollment.byu.edu/enrollment-services-counselors*
Phone: (801) 422-4104
Email: admissions@byu.edu

COST OF ATTENDANCE:

Tuition & Fees: $12,240 | **Additional Expenses:** $14,036
Total: $26,276

*Note: BYU is affiliated with the Church of Jesus Christ of Latter-day Saints. Students who are affiliated with the Church have lower costs (Tuition: $6,120, COA: $20,156).

Financial Aid: https://enrollment.byu.edu/financialaid

ADDITIONAL INFORMATION:

Available Degree(s)

- BFA Photo- & Lens-Based Design

Portfolio Requirement

Portfolios are not required for incoming students. Applicants select Pre-Photography as their major. After passing a portfolio review in the first year, students may then move onto pre-BFA status. After the pre-BFA status, they may apply once again with a portfolio to the full BFA program.

Scholarships Offered

Freshman scholarships are merit-based and include the Russell M. Nelson Scholarship (150% of Latter-day Saints Tuition for 8 semesters), the Sterling Scholarship Competition (for UT high school seniors), and the National Merit Scholarship (for National Merit finalists). In addition, international students are eligible for academic, merit-based scholarships.

Special Opportunities

Students in the BFA Photo & Lens-Based Design program must complete an internship during their undergraduate years. They are also required to complete a capstone project that is an individual project on photography within a topic of their choice.

Notable Alumni

Don Bluth, Jeremy Coon, C. Jay Cox, Mitch Davis, Richard Dutcher, Aaron Eckhart, Neil LaBute, Aaron Ruell, Reed P. Smoot, and Daryn Tufts

UNIVERSITY OF WASHINGTON

Address: University of Washington, Seattle, WA 98195
Website: *https://art.washington.edu/art/ba-art-photomedia-concentration*
Contact: *https://admit.washington.edu/contact/*
Phone: (206) 543-9686
Email: Contact via contact link.

COST OF ATTENDANCE:

In-State Tuition & Fees: $12,076 | **Additional Expenses:** $18,564
Total: $30,640

Out-of-State Tuition & Fees: $39,906 | **Additional Expenses:** $18,564
Total: $58,470

Financial Aid: https://www.washington.edu/financialaid/

ADDITIONAL INFORMATION:

Available Degree(s)

- BA Art, concentration: Photo/Media

Portfolio Requirement

There is no portfolio requirement for incoming students.

Scholarships Offered

UW offers several types of institutional aid for all students. Washington residents that show exceptional leadership and community engagement may be eligible for the Presidential Scholarship (valued at $10,000). All U.S. citizens may be eligible for the Purple & Gold Scholarship. High-need, high achieving students are eligible for the UW Diversity Scholarship ($10,000 per year for four years).

Special Opportunities

UW houses facilities such as two experimental galleries, a black-and-white darkroom, large printers, computer labs, a sound studio, and more. Photo/Media students learn about techniques in contemporary art, particularly in photography, video, mixed media, and installation. Students learn historical perspectives as well.

Notable Alumni

Imogen Cunningham, Martina López, and Art Wolfe

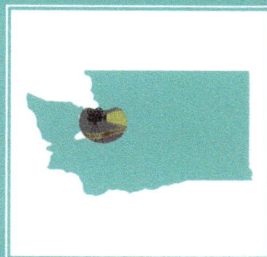

ALASKA

ARIZONA

CALIFORNIA

COLORADO

HAWAII

IDAHO

MONTANA

NEVADA

NEW MEXICO

OREGON

UTAH

WASHINGTON

WYOMING

WEST

CHAPTER 14

PHOTOGRAPHY SCHOOLS BY CITY/ STATE

School	City	State
Arizona State University	Tempe	Arizona
Pacific Union College	Angwin	California
California State University, Long Beach	Long Beach	California
Fashion Institute of Design and Merchandising	Los Angeles	California
ArtCenter College of Design	Pasadena	California
California State University, Sacramento	Sacramento	California
Academy of Art University	San Francisco	California
California College of the Arts	San Francisco	California
California Institute of the Arts	Valencia	California
The George Washington University	Washington	DC
University of Miami	Coral Gables	Florida
University of Central Florida	Orlando	Florida
Savannah College of Art and Design	Savannah	Georgia
University of Illinois, Urbana-Champaign	Champaign	Illinois
Columbia College Chicago	Chicago	Illinois
School of the Art Institute Chicago	Chicago	Illinois
Purdue University	West Lafayette	Indiana
University of Iowa	Iowa City	Iowa
Western Kentucky University	Bowling Green	Kentucky
Louisiana Tech University	Ruston	Louisiana
Maryland Institute College of Art	Baltimore	Maryland
Massachusetts College of Art & Design	Boston	Massachusetts
Washington University, St. Louis	St. Louis	Missouri
Pratt Institute	Brooklyn	New York
SUNY Buffalo	Buffalo	New York
Fashion Institute of Technology	New York	New York
New York University	New York	New York
Parsons School of Design	New York	New York
School of Visual Arts	New York	New York
St. John's University	Queens	New York
Rochester Institute of Technology	Rochester	New York
Syracuse University	Syracuse	New York
Ohio University	Athens	Ohio

School	City	State
Cleveland Institute of Art	Cleveland	Ohio
Columbus College of Art & Design	Columbus	Ohio
University of Dayton	Dayton	Ohio
Kent State University	Kent	Ohio
University of Central Oklahoma	Edmond	Oklahoma
University of Oregon	Eugene	Oregon
Drexel University	Philadelphia	Pennsylvania
Temple University	Philadelphia	Pennsylvania
University of the Arts	Philadelphia	Pennsylvania
Providence College	Providence	Rhode Island
Rhode Island School of Design	Providence	Rhode Island
Texas Christian University	Fort Worth	Texas
University of Houston	Houston	Texas
Sam Houston State University	Huntsville	Texas
Texas State University	San Marcos	Texas
Brigham Young University	Provo	Utah
Virginia Commonwealth University	Richmond	Virginia
University of Washington	Seattle	Washington

CHAPTER 16

PHOTOGRAPHY SCHOOLS BY AVERAGE TEST SCORE

School	Avg. SAT
Pacific Union College	460-580 (ERW) 440-560 (M)
California State University, Sacramento	470-570 (ERW) 460-560 (M)
Sam Houston State University	490-570 (ERW) 480-550 (M)
Western Kentucky University	500-600 (ERW) 480-580 (M)
Texas State University	510-600 (ERW) 500-580 (M)
Kent State University	510-610 (ERW) 510-600 (M)
California State University, Long Beach	510-620 (ERW) 510-620 (M)
Ohio University	530-630 (ERW) 520-620 (M)
Louisiana Tech University	530-640 (ERW) 530-630 (M)
Savannah College of Art and Design	540-640 (ERW) 500-600 (M)
Virginia Commonwealth University	540-640 (ERW) 520-610 (M)
St. John's University	540-640 (ERW) 540-660 (M)
University of Dayton	540-640 (ERW) 540-660 (M)
School of Visual Arts	545-650 (ERW) 530-680 (M)
University of Oregon	550-650 (ERW) 540-640 (M)
Arizona State University	550-650 (ERW) 550-670 (M)
	*Test-optional
SUNY Buffalo	560-640 (ERW) 580-670 (M)
University of Houston	560-650 (ERW) 560-660 (M)
School of the Art Institute Chicago	560-660 (ERW) 480-600 (M)
Texas Christian University	560-660 (ERW) 550-660 (M)
Cleveland Institute of Art	560-680 (ERW) 510-620 (M)
Pratt Institute	570-660 (ERW) 550-680 (M)
University of Iowa	570-680 (ERW) 560-670 (M)
Parsons School of Design	580-680 (ERW) 560-680 (M)
Drexel University	590-680 (ERW) 590-700 (M)
Purdue University	590-690 (ERW) 600-740 (M)
University of Washington	590-700 (ERW) 610-753 (M)
University of Illinois, Urbana-Champaign	590-700 (ERW) 620-770 (M)
University of Central Florida	600-680 (ERW) 570-670 (M)
Rochester Institute of Technology	600-690 (ERW) 620-730 (M)
Providence College	610-680 (ERW) 600-680 (M)
Rhode Island School of Design	610-700 (ERW) 640-770 (M)
Brigham Young University	610-700 (ERW) 590-710 (M)
University of Miami	620-700 (ERW) 630-720 (M)
The George Washington University	640-720 (ERW) 630-730 (M)
New York University	670-740 (ERW) 700-800 (M)

School	Avg. SAT
Washington University, St. Louis	720-760 (ERW) 760-800 (M)
Syracuse University	N/A
University of Central Oklahoma	N/A
Academy of Art University	N/A *Open Admissions
ArtCenter College of Design	N/A *Test optional
California College of the Arts	N/A *Test optional
California Institute of the Arts	N/A *Test optional
Columbia College Chicago	N/A *Test optional
Columbus College of Art & Design	N/A *Test optional
Fashion Institute of Design and Merchandising	N/A *Test optional
Fashion Institute of Technology	N/A *Test optional
Maryland Institute College of Art	N/A *Test optional
Massachusetts College of Art & Design	N/A *Test optional
Temple University	N/A *Test optional
University of the Arts	N/A *Test optional

PHOTOGRAPHY SCHOOLS BY AVERAGE ACT SCORE

School	Avg. ACT C
California State University, Sacramento	17-23
Pacific Union College	17-24
Sam Houston State University	18-23
University of Central Oklahoma	18-24
Western Kentucky University	19-26
Cleveland Institute of Art	19-27
Texas State University	20-25
California State University, Long Beach	20-26
Kent State University	20-26
Savannah College of Art and Design	20-27
Ohio University	21-26
Virginia Commonwealth University	21-28
Arizona State University	21-28 *Test-optional
School of the Art Institute Chicago	22-25
Louisiana Tech University	22-28
University of Houston	22-28
University of Iowa	22-29

School	Avg. ACT C
University of Oregon	22-29
School of Visual Arts	23-27
St. John's University	23-29
SUNY Buffalo	23-29
University of Dayton	23-29
Pratt Institute	25-30
University of Central Florida	25-30
Drexel University	25-31
Texas Christian University	25-31
Purdue University	25-33
Parsons School of Design	26-30
Brigham Young University	26-32
Providence College	27-31
Rhode Island School of Design	27-32
University of Illinois, Urbana-Champaign	27-33
University of Washington	27-33
University of Miami	28-32
Rochester Institute of Technology	28-33
The George Washington University	29-33
New York University	31-34
Washington University, St. Louis	33-35
Syracuse University	N/A
Academy of Art University	N/A *Open Admissions
ArtCenter College of Design	N/A *Test optional
California College of the Arts	N/A *Test optional
California Institute of the Arts	N/A *Test optional
Columbia College Chicago	N/A *Test optional
Columbus College of Art & Design	N/A *Test optional
Fashion Institute of Design and Merchandising	N/A *Test optional
Fashion Institute of Technology	N/A *Test optional
Maryland Institute College of Art	N/A *Test optional
Massachusetts College of Art & Design	N/A *Test optional
Temple University	N/A *Test optional
University of the Arts	N/A *Test optional

PHOTOGRAPHY SCHOOLS BY AVERAGE GPA

School	Avg. GPA
California State University, Sacramento	3.41
Western Kentucky University	3.44
Temple University	3.48
Ohio University	3.55
Louisiana Tech University	3.56
Savannah College of Art and Design	3.6
University of Miami	3.6
Kent State University	3.61
University of Oregon	3.65
Purdue University	3.67
Syracuse University	3.67
California State University, Long Beach	3.68
Rochester Institute of Technology	3.7
SUNY Buffalo	3.7
New York University	3.71
Virginia Commonwealth University	3.72
University of Dayton	3.73
University of Houston	3.73
University of Iowa	3.81
Pratt Institute	3.82
University of Washington	3.82
Brigham Young University	3.86
University of Central Florida	4.16
Washington University, St. Louis	4.21
Arizona State University	N/A
ArtCenter College of Design	N/A
California College of the Arts	N/A
California Institute of the Arts	N/A
Cleveland Institute of Art	N/A
Columbia College Chicago	N/A
Columbus College of Art & Design	N/A
Drexel University	N/A
Fashion Institute of Design and Merchandising	N/A
Fashion Institute of Technology	N/A
Maryland Institute College of Art	N/A
Massachusetts College of Art & Design	N/A

School	Avg. GPA
Pacific Union College	N/A
Parsons School of Design	N/A
Providence College	N/A
Rhode Island School of Design	N/A
Sam Houston State University	N/A
School of the Art Institute Chicago	N/A
School of Visual Arts	N/A
St. John's University	N/A
Texas Christian University	N/A
Texas State University	N/A
The George Washington University	N/A
University of Central Oklahoma	N/A
University of Illinois, Urbana-Champaign	N/A
University of the Arts	N/A
Academy of Art University	N/A *Open Admissions

CHAPTER 17

LEADING PHOTOGRAPHY PROGRAMS

TOP TWELVE UNDERGRADUATE PHOTOGRAPHY PROGRAMS

1. Rhode Island School of Design
2. Parsons School of Design
3. School of the Art Institute of Chicago
4. Rochester Institute of Technology
5. New York University
6. Syracuse University
7. George Washington University
8. California Institute of the Arts
9. Washington University in St. Louis
10. Columbia College Chicago
11. University of Miami
12. University of Washington, Seattle

TOP TEN FASHION PHOTOGRAPHY COLLEGES

1. Parson's School of Design
2. Rhode Island School of Design
3. Royal College of Art
4. New York University
5. Paris College of Art
6. Accademia Italiana
7. Fashion Institute of Technology
8. California Institute of the Arts
9. School of the Art Inst. of Chicago
10. Columbia College Chicago

TOP TWENTY FASHION PHOTOGRAPHERS

1. Edward Steichen
2. George Hoyningen-Huene
3. Cecil Beaton
4. Clarence Hudson White
5. Tim Walker
6. Steven Klein
7. Steven Meisel
8. Norman Parkinson
9. Horst P. Horst
10. Lee Miller
11. Richard Avedon
12. Guy Bourdin
13. Helmut Newton
14. Irvine Penn
15. David Bailey
16. Patrick Demarchelier
17. Annie Leibovitz
18. Mario Testino
19. Lara Jade
20. Peter Lindbergh

TOP TEN PHOTOJOURNALISM COLLEGES

1. George Washington University
2. Syracuse University
3. University of the Arts London
4. Rochester Inst. of Tech.
5. Boston University
6. Central Michigan University
7. Ohio University
8. Western Kentucky University
9. Kent State University
10. University of Central Oklahoma

TOP TEN GRADUATE SCHOOL PHOTOGRAPHY PROGRAMS

1. Yale University
2. University of California, Los Angeles
3. Rhode Island School of Design
4. School of the Art Institute of Chicago
5. University of Arizona
6. Arizona State University
7. Rochester Inst. of Tech.
8. University of New Mexico
9. Bard College
10. California Institute of the Arts

CHAPTER 18

TOP U.S. & INTERNATIONAL ART PROGRAMS

U.S. – ACCREDITED COLLEGES FOCUSED ON ART

United States

Art Academy of Cincinnati (OH)

ArtCenter College of Design (CA)

Art Institute of Boston (MA)

Art Institute of Pittsburgh (PA)

California College of the Arts (CA)

California Institute of the Arts (CA)

Cleveland Institute of Art (OH)

College for Creative Studies (MI)

Columbia College Chicago (IL)

Cooper Union (NY)

Corcoran Col. of Art & Design - GWU (DC)

Cornish College of the Arts (WA)

Fashion Institute of Technology (NY)

Kansas City Art Institute (MO)

Kendall College of Art & Design (MI)

Laguna College of Art & Design (CA)

Lyme Academy College of Fine Arts (CT)

Maine College of Art (ME)

Maryland Institute College of Art (MD)

Mass. College of Art & Design (MA)

Memphis College of Art (TN)

Milwaukee Institute of Art & Design (WI)

Minneapolis College of Art & Design (MN)

Montserrat College of Art (MA)

Moore College of Art & Design (PA)

New Hampshire Institute of Art (NH)

N. Michigan Univ. School of Art & Design (MI)

Oregon College of Art & Craft (OR)

Otis College of Art & Design (CA)

Pacific Northwest College of Art (OR)

Parsons School of Design (NY)

Pratt Institute (NY)

Rhode Island School of Design (RI)

Ringling College of Art & Design (FL)

San Francisco Art Institute (CA)

Savannah College of Art & Design (GA)

School of the Art Institute of Chicago (IL)

School of the Museum of Fine Arts (MA)

Vermont College of Fine Arts (VT)

Watkins College of Art, Design, & Film (TN)

U.S. – ACCREDITED COLLEGES FOCUSED ON ART

International

Adelaide Central School of Art (Australia)

Alberta University of the Arts (Canada)

Bauhaus University Weimar (Germany)

Camberwell College of Arts (England)

Emily Carr Univ. of Art & Design (Canada)

Government College of Art & Craft (India)

Grekov Odessa Art School (Ukraine)

National Art School (Australia)

Nova Scotia College of Art & Design Univ. (Canada)

Ontario College of Art & Design Univ. (Canada)

Paris College of Art (France)

2021 QS RANKED TOP UNIVERSITIES FOR PHOTOGRAPHY WORLDWIDE

1. Royal College of Art (U.K.)
2. University of the Arts London (U.K.)
3. Parsons School of Design (NY-USA)
4. Rhode Island School of Design (RI-USA)
5. Massachusetts Institute of Technology (MA-USA)
6. Politecnico de Milano (Italy)
7. Aalto University (Finland)
8. School of the Art Institute of Chicago (IL-USA)
9. Glasgow School of Art (U.K.)
10. Pratt Institute (NY-USA)
11. ArtCenter College of Design (CA-USA)
12. Delft University of Technology (Netherlands)
13. Design Academy Eindhoven (Netherlands)
14. Tongji University (China)
15. Goldsmiths, University of London (U.K.)
16. Royal Melbourne Institute of Technology (Australia)
17. California Institute of the Arts (CA-USA)
18. Carnegie Mellon University (PA-USA)
19. Stanford University (CA-USA)
20. Hong Kong Polytechnic University (H.K. SAR)

JOURNEY TO ART, DANCE, MUSIC, THEATRE, FILM, AND FASHION SERIES

JOURNEY TO
Fashion Design
COLLEGE ADMISSIONS & PROFILES

RACHEL A. WINSTON, PH.D.

JOURNEY TO
Fashion Merchandising
COLLEGE ADMISSIONS & PROFILES

RACHEL A. WINSTON, PH.D.

JOURNEY TO
Costume Design & Technical Theatre
COLLEGE ADMISSIONS & PROFILES

RACHEL A. WINSTON, PH.D.

JOURNEY TO
Theatre and the Dramatic Arts
COLLEGE ADMISSIONS & PROFILES

RACHEL A. WINSTON, PH.D.

JOURNEY TO *Musical* **Theatre**
COLLEGE ADMISSIONS & PROFILES

RACHEL A. WINSTON, PH.D.

JOURNEY TO *Architecture*
COLLEGE ADMISSIONS & PROFILES

RACHEL A. WINSTON, PH.D.

Live your dreams today remembering that discipline is the bridge between dreams and achievement!

"We believe in the American Dream that all people rich or poor can go as far in life as their talents and persistence will take them."
– Lizard Publishing Vision

At Lizard, we help you make your dreams come true.

CONTACT INFORMATION

Phone: 949-833-7706

E-mail: collegeguide@yahoo.com

Website: collegelizard.com and Lizard-publishing.com

COMPREHENSIVE HEALTH CARE SERIES

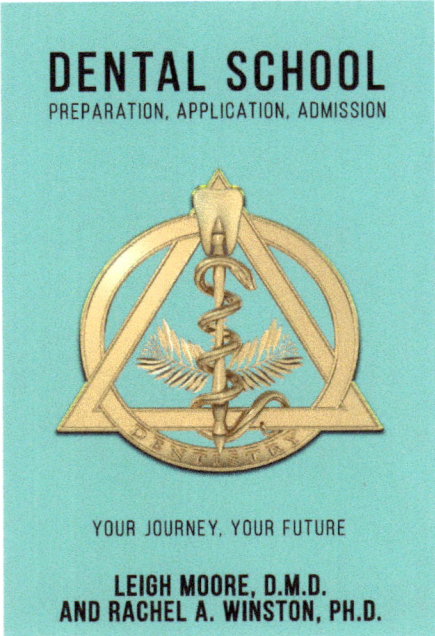

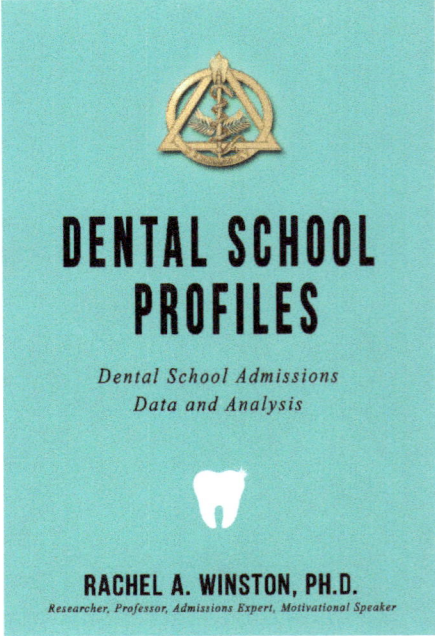

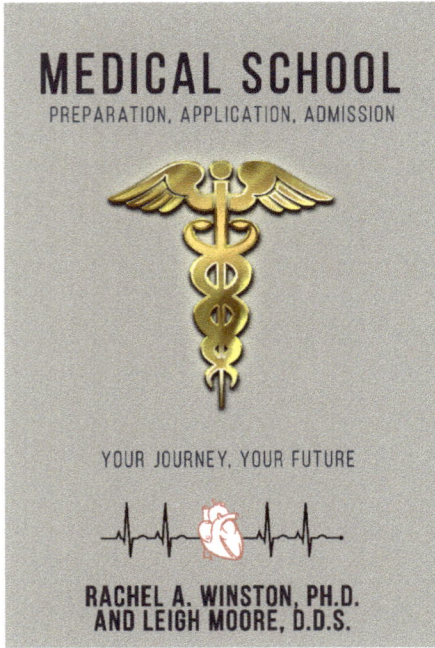

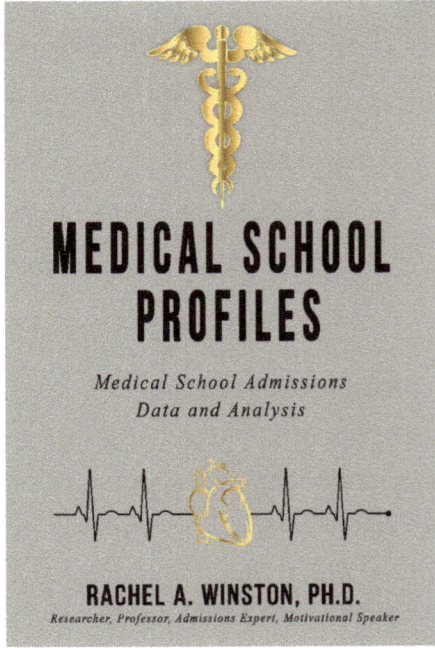

DENTAL SCHOOL
PREPARATION, APPLICATION, ADMISSION

YOUR JOURNEY, YOUR FUTURE

**LEIGH MOORE, D.M.D.
AND RACHEL A. WINSTON, PH.D.**

DENTAL SCHOOL PROFILES

*Dental School Admissions
Data and Analysis*

RACHEL A. WINSTON, PH.D.
Researcher, Professor, Admissions Expert, Motivational Speaker

MEDICAL SCHOOL
PREPARATION, APPLICATION, ADMISSION

YOUR JOURNEY, YOUR FUTURE

**RACHEL A. WINSTON, PH.D.
AND LEIGH MOORE, D.D.S.**

MEDICAL SCHOOL PROFILES

*Medical School Admissions
Data and Analysis*

RACHEL A. WINSTON, PH.D.
Researcher, Professor, Admissions Expert, Motivational Speaker

VET SCHOOL
PREPARATION, APPLICATION, ADMISSION

YOUR JOURNEY, YOUR FUTURE

RACHEL A. WINSTON, PH.D.
Researcher, Professor, Admissions Expert, Motivational Speaker

VET SCHOOL PROFILES

Veterinary Medical School Admissions Data and Analysis

RACHEL A. WINSTON, PH.D.
Researcher, Professor, Admissions Expert, Motivational Speaker

PHYSICIAN ASST. (PA) SCHOOL
PREPARATION, APPLICATION, ADMISSION

YOUR JOURNEY, YOUR FUTURE

RACHEL A. WINSTON, PH.D.
Researcher, Professor, Admissions Expert, Motivational Speaker

PHYSICIAN ASST. SCHOOL PROFILES

P.A. School Admissions Data and Analysis

RACHEL A. WINSTON, PH.D.
Researcher, Professor, Admissions Expert, Motivational Speaker

PHARM.D. SCHOOL
PREPARATION, APPLICATION, ADMISSION

YOUR JOURNEY, YOUR FUTURE

RACHEL A. WINSTON, PH.D.
Researcher, Professor, Admissions Expert, Motivational Speaker

PHARM.D. SCHOOL PROFILES

Pharmacy School Admissions Data and Analysis

RACHEL A. WINSTON, PH.D.
Researcher, Professor, Admissions Expert, Motivational Speaker

OSTEOPATHIC MEDICAL SCHOOL
PREPARATION, APPLICATION, ADMISSION

YOUR JOURNEY, YOUR FUTURE

RACHEL A. WINSTON, PH.D.
Researcher, Professor, Admissions Expert, Motivational Speaker

OSTEO SCHOOL PROFILES

Osteopathic Medical School Admissions Data and Analysis

RACHEL A. WINSTON, PH.D.
Researcher, Professor, Admissions Expert, Motivational Speaker

Is Medical School Your Goal?
FROM
HIGH SCHOOL
TO
MEDICAL SCHOOL

The Ultimate Guide to
BS/MD Programs

Rachel A. Winston, Ph.D.
Researcher, Professor, Admissions Expert, Motivational Speaker

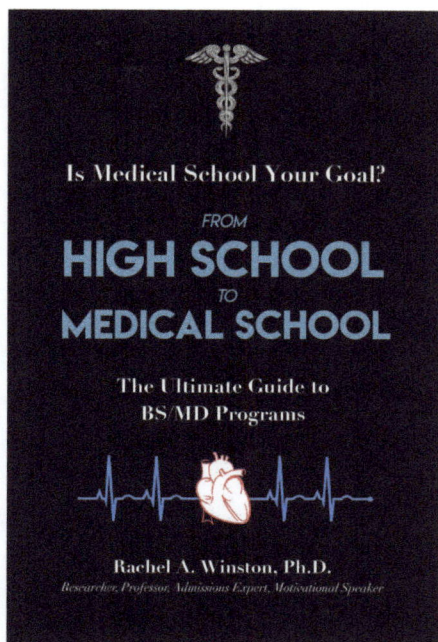

This comprehensive healthcare series is designed in full color to aid the growing number of applicants seeking clear, comprehensive materials. As a college admissions expert and former UCLA College Counseling Certificate Program faculty member, Dr. Winston is dedicated to helping students obtain the information they need.

FOR MORE INFORMATION

bsmdguide.com

medschoolexpert.com

Purchase books at Lizard-publishing.com

SERVICES OFFERED BY LIZARD EDUCATION:

- College Counseling
- Admissions News/Resources
- Essay Support and Editing
- Interview Preparation
- Road Trips to Visit Colleges
- Career Planning/Majors/Resumes
- BS/MD, BS/DO, BS/JD, BS/DDS
- Medical School
- Graduate School (Masters & Doctorate)
- Film Studio and Editing
- Portfolio Assistance/SlideRoom
- Athletics Recruiting/Highlight Films
- International Admissions/Visa/TOEFL
- Financial Aid and Scholarships
- UCs, Ivy Leagues, and Colleges Nationwide
- Book Publishing
- Engineering, Robotics, STEM
- Art Portfolios

Email: collegeguide@yahoo.com
Website: collegelizard.com

LIZARD

INDEX

Symbols

A

C

D

E

F

G

H

I

N

O

S

V

W

Y

Z

www.ingramcontent.com/pod-product-compliance
Lightning Source LLC
Chambersburg PA
CBHW052017030426
42335CB00026B/3181